7/7: Muslim Perspectives

RABITA

Published by Rabita

Rabita Limited
PO Box 601
Northolt,
UB5 9NY
UK

www.rabita.org.uk

First published July 2010

British Library Cataloguing-in-Publication Data

ISBN 978-0-9565967-0-3

I. London Terrorist Bombings, London, England, 2005 -- Social aspects. 2. Muslims -- Non-Muslim countries -- Attitudes. 3. Muslims -- Non-Muslim countries -- Social conditions -- 21st century. 4. Terrorism -- Religious aspects -- Islam.

I. Seven/seven II. Shibli, Murtaza.

303.6'25'088297-dc22

Typesetting and cover design by Muhammad Amin, Norwich

Printed in Great Britain by the MPG Books Group, Bodmin and King's Lynn

7/7: Muslim Perspectives

Edited by

Murtaza Shibli

ENDORSEMENTS

"This book ...tells how the lives of people who had no connection whatever with those events, were stained or scarred by them, and how they have made their accommodation with a country in which suddenly, one day in early summer, life suddenly changed, and they became aware of themselves, their sense of belonging, their place and their future in ways which they had never dreamed. These are powerful accounts from the heart."

- Jeremy Seabrook, Author, 'The Refuge and the Fortress'

"7/7: Muslim Perspectives is an important contribution that should be read by everyone who was affected by 7/7. While the collection highlights the heterogeneous nature of Muslims in Britain it does nevertheless highlight the extent to which popularist accounts of the significance of the bombers' Muslim identities has had the adverse consequence of stigmatising all Muslims as terrorists and extremists."

- Robert Lambert MBE, University of Exeter
Co-author, 'Islamophobia and Anti-Muslim Hate Crime: a London Case Study'

"Forgoing the anecdotal or statistical evidence that has until now dominated studies of how UK Muslims have adapted to the post-9/11 world, Murtaza Shibli's book places the bombings within narratives that give them both a social context and intellectual depth. This is a work that will be of significance for journalists as well as academics, and those involved in politics and policing alike."

- Faisal Devji, St. Antony's College, Oxford University,
Author, 'Landscapes of Jihad'

"At first sight, what we note here are responses that the vast majority of us recall only too well from that fateful day: shock, anxiety about the safety of loved ones, the apparently absurd rupture to the normality of everyday life, the abiding fears about what lies ahead. On closer look, however, this volume also reveals the subtle but menacing ways in which a significant minority of innocent citizens have become insinuated through no fault of their own in global antagonisms to the detriment of their dignity and peace of mind. Not only do British Muslims, like all British citizens, have to live with the trauma of 7/7: that alone is bad enough. They also must then live with the frame of 'terrorist,' potential if not definite, that has come to be placed on them."

- Parvati Nair, Director, Centre for the Study of Migration,
Queen Mary, University of London

"Revealing a wide range of experiences and attitudes, the contributors provide insights into a cross-section of Muslim society in Britain today... However, the picture is not all rosy and many of the contributors question some of the actions and initiatives of the government following 7/7. Their concerns challenge both government and society."

- Dr. John Chesworth, The Centre for Muslim Christian Studies, Oxford

"With memories of 7/7 still very much vivid five years on, this collection of narratives offers a poignant reminder of the feelings of grief, shame, and bewilderment many British Muslims experienced that day – to a degree most non-Muslims never realised.... [T]he reader cannot but be impressed by the vigor and the determination to self-introspection displayed throughout the book in order to regain confidence and to challenge the fringe groups of extremists that hijacked existing grievances and violently politicised Islam. A clear message of genuine hope rings loud and clear: that one day all Britain might borrow from Pete Seeger and proudly hum: 'This Land was Made for You and Me'."

- Rik Coolsaet, Ghent University, Belgium,
Member, European Commission Expert Group on Violent Radicalisation

7/7: Muslim Perspectives

This book explores and articulates insights, reactions and experiences of a wide range of Muslim men and women following the events of 7/7 – their feelings, anxieties and concerns. Also how they negotiated their own position with mainstream society and with each other in the aftermath. They reflect on the event and express their personal response, serving as a starting point for an exploration of the challenges and expectations which the future holds for them.

As the contributors come from diverse cultural and professional backgrounds, and a wide variety of spiritual practices, this project offers a rich mosaic of lived experience, subjective accounts of people's hopes, worries and fears. In doing so, it offers a deeper meaning and understanding of Muslim lives in this country. It serves equally to put into perspective Islamic extremist ideologies in fringe groups.

The book offers a compelling range of testimony to those with an interest in the lives of Muslims – students, journalists, politicians, policy makers, academics etc. It gives a voice to Muslims who are rarely heard, and an opportunity to disseminate those voices in such a way as to promote cross-cultural bonds and amity.

Murtaza Shibli

Murtaza Shibli is a trainer, writer and consultant on Muslim issues, security and conflict, and expert on South Asia. He has worked as a journalist, security consultant and aid worker. In his recent role, he worked for the Muslim Council of Britain as Public Affairs and Media Officer.

As a journalist in Kashmir, he has campaigned for minority Hindu rights and spent time with scores of guerrilla resistance leaders and interviewed them along with some Afghan jihad veterans. He has written a monograph on Hizbul Mujahideen, the largest guerilla resistance group in Kashmir which was added to European Union's terrorist organisations in December 2005.

He has an MA in Mass Communication and Journalism from the University of Kashmir and MSc. in Violence, Conflict and Development from the School of Oriental and African Studies (SOAS), University of London.

He is also a poet and a song writer, and is currently working on his first music album in his mother tongue – Koshur.

TO LONDON
& ITS SPIRIT

The greatest tribute that we can pay to the deceased is to overcome the hatred and division that the killers sought to foment.

ACKNOWLEDGEMENTS

I WOULD like to thank all of the contributors for sharing their experiences and thoughts on a subject that is very sensitive. My special thanks go to Jeremy Seabrook, author and commentator, and Mohammed Amin for their continuous support and instruction. I would also like to acknowledge the support from John Chesworth of the Centre for Muslim Christian Studies, Oxford; Amina Rawat and Hasan Ahmed for their generous and constructive comments. My thanks are due to Canon Guy Wilkinson, National Inter-Religious Affairs Advisor & Secretary for Inter-Religious Affairs to the Archbishop of Canterbury; Robert Lambert of the University of Exeter and Parvati Nair, Director, Centre for Migration Studies, Queen Mary University of London for their support. I am also grateful to Muhammad Amin for layout and cover design. My profound thanks go to my wife, Afiyah Rai, who has supported this project and believed in its value. Since my previous employment at the Muslim Council of Britain, I have been totally devoted to this project, not bringing any money home; something my wife understood and patiently endured. I am also thankful to my parents-in-law, Savinder and Jaspal Rai, who looked after my one year old son, Sulaiman, while I worked on this book.

Contents

Open Your Eyes

The time is here, stand tall and be counted

Shield young minds and stop them from being clouded

We must face these so called martyrs falling

To protect the innocent there is no time for stalling

The struggle is here together as one we must be

We cannot falter in the face of this new enemy

Don't be fooled, the most trusted are ever so tricksy and wise

They will take your liberties and disappear in to the dark skies

Take your loved ones and forever break with you their ties

Be warned, the enemy is among us, now open your eyes.

Ahmed Bashir

INTRODUCTION

THE tragedy of 7/7 was not unique in its method or in the terror it sought to instil, any more than the regular massacres of innocent civilians in the wars which 24 hour television has brought into our living rooms. What was particularly shocking for all of us in the UK was the fact that the perpetrators were not outsiders, but home grown, born and brought up in the UK. The tragedy nonetheless redefined and re-focussed the way Muslims are seen and perceived, but perhaps more poignantly also redefined the way Muslims see themselves.

In the five years since the events of 7/7, Islamophobia and anti-Muslim violence in Britain have grown disproportionately and become increasingly acceptable within mainstream culture. There have been a record number of reported assaults on Muslim men and women, desecration of Muslim graves, vandalism against Mosques, schools and even Muslim charity shops. This also seems to have undermined the confidence of common, law-abiding Muslims, whose daily life struggles are compounded by society's demand that they identify, fight and root out the extremists and terrorists within. While undertaking research for this publication, I learned of a moving incident from a Metropolitan Police community outreach officer which typifies the prevailing, scarcely acknowledged, atmosphere. Having noticed his nine-year old son showing signs of unease and worry, he decided to check up on him. Upon entering his son's room, after a few affectionate remarks, the son turned to his dad and enquired, "Dad...it is only Muslims who can become terrorists...innit?" In today's Britain, negative characterisations also permeate the imagination of young children; a reality to which many Muslim school children in playgrounds are accustomed.

This book was born out of my own personal relationship with the terror of violence and conflict. As a Kashmiri born on the Indian side of Kashmir, I was surrounded by death and disorder as a teenager and, later, as a journalist, watched the dance of death almost every day. I lost scores of my close friends, relatives and neighbours to violence perpetrated by the Indian army, who claimed to defend us, and by the Kashmiri militia groups, who claimed to fight for our dignity as a nation or in the name of Islam to protect us from the advances of an 'infidel' Indian army. Scores of others died in internecine fighting amongst the militia groups, again in the name of Islam or the dignity of the people of Kashmir. Many of the arguments that were used to justify the 7/7 atrocity were present in Kashmir. My personal response to 7/7 was more harrowing because I saw my own vulnerability played out again in London, which I had constructed in my mind as a fortress against the thoughts and experiences I had been subjected to earlier in Kashmir. As I discuss in my contribution, 'Reliving the Past' (page 65), I felt humiliated by my own naivety, naivety which slowly grew into frustration as British Muslims suffered in silence; a frustration created by fringe elements which were granted supposed leadership status by a section of the media that was out to discredit the majority of Muslims by whipping up passion through stereotypes of 'Angry Muslims'.

This project articulates the reflections of ordinary Muslims in the UK who come from different professional and cultural backgrounds. Apart from a word limit, I gave the contributors freedom to express in their own words their experiences and thoughts on the day of the attack, and their experiences and reflections in its aftermath. Some who were approached refused outright to contribute, while others displayed their discomfort about the subject. Their reasons for refusing varied; some feared it might attract adverse interest from the security services, others appeared worn down by the continuing media focus which risks stigmatising all Muslims as terrorists or terrorist sympathisers. The greatest reluctance to contribute was encountered in young male Muslims, many of whom feared being spied upon. A Muslim woman teacher bluntly asked if this exercise had anything to do with the intelligence agencies. She refused to contribute as she thought it was part of the Government's counterterrorism strategy Preventing Violent Extremism (Prevent), and therefore most likely to be a 'monitoring' project.

The end result shows the diversity of political and religious views arising from 7/7 and its repercussions. However, readers should remember that contributors were chosen because they were capable of writing fluently in English, so there is no representation from Muslims who lack this skill. Unlike an opinion poll, there is no attempt to weigh the representation for Muslim demographics. On the other hand, one can get inside the mind of the contributor in a way that is completely impossible with polls or fragments transcribed during focus group sessions.

Half the contributors in this collection are women. This was to ensure that the perspectives of Muslim women were not only heard, but also that their anxieties about their children, their families and their lives were articulated. Among the contributors are immigrants, who have lived or are living in the UK as students or workers. These immigrants form a very important part of Muslim social life and play a very significant role in shaping its discourse and responses. In addition, this collection contains accounts by four white English converts, both men and women, who are sometimes referred to as reverts.[1] From my years of contact with them, there is a general unease among many 'reverts' at being left out of the 'Muslim discourse' both by the government and by the immigrant originated Muslim communities who outnumber them. I have come across this feeling among many white Muslims, that the government is chasing 'exotic' Muslims who look different and can therefore easily tick the boxes in the government's agenda on race and religion.

As I worked through the contributions, I found myself continuously reflecting upon the wider social significance of 7/7. The most painful aspect of the attack was that it was carried out by British citizens, either born or raised in this country, and not by foreign terrorists. The pain was amplified for British Muslims by the fact that the terrorists were Muslims and claimed to be acting in the name of Islam; as contributor after contributor points out, Islam prohibits such mass murder. In my view, the contradiction between the actions of the terrorists and the religious beliefs of the Muslim population is so painful that it drives some to 7/7 denial, so that the attacks are blamed on others in a manner typical of conspiracy theories. It goes without saying that those in the forefront of saving our capital and the country from similar atrocities include hundreds of dedicated Muslim police officers and community members across the country. These faceless heroes have provided, and still do, a tremendous contribution without having been recognised, either individually or as a community.

---

1 When a non-Muslim embraces Islam, Muslims call it 'reversion' rather than conversion, as they consider all children are initially born into the state of Islam. This is based upon sayings of the Prophet Muhammad (peace be upon him).

Some of the readers of this book may feel that overall it reflects an 'apologist' tone from Muslims as presented in many of the pieces. This has to be seen as a natural reaction to the continuous frenzy whipped against Muslims without any appreciation of the diversity of their political beliefs or spiritual practice and ideology. Many contributors feel that they have to redeem Islam in the eyes of the mainstream, and this imposes a terrible burden upon them. As is evident from various contributions, many Muslims feel they have to propitiate other people's prejudice and ignorance, almost an impossible task to achieve under the current circumstances. Muslims overwhelmingly reject terror as a means of achieving political goals – every Muslim group of any standing condemned 7/7 without any reservations. Unfortunately the media have failed to give sufficient prominence to such condemnations, and often 'counterbalance' them with statements from wholly unrepresentative fringe groups which support terrorism or extremism, leaving the British public confused about what British Muslims actually believe.

The media are also too quick to forget that eight Muslims died on 7/7; four murderers but also four innocent Muslim victims who are included in the total of 52 victims. While the Muslim identity of the bombers is always emphasised, most of the Muslim victims of 7/7 have been denied their religious identity. As a result, the media have consistently downplayed the existence of Muslim victims. While people know that Shahara Akhter Islam (20, from Plaistow, East London, a bank cashier) was a devout Muslim, there is rarely similar acknowledgement for the three other 7/7 Muslim victims – Atique Sharifi, 24, an Afghan national who was living in Hounslow, Middlesex; Ihab Slimane, a 24-year-old IT graduate from Lyon, France; and Gamze Günoral, 24, a Turkish student.

I hope this collection will provoke fresh thinking as to how our media and politicians can redefine their perceptions of Muslim communities in our country, perceptions that have become ossified in recent times, thanks to the harrowing imagery associated with 'the actions of Muslims', particularly any violent activities. There are the beginnings of a paradigm shift in rhetoric, with the emergence of the new United States Obama administration – one more willing to entertain the common humanity of Muslims. Unfortunately such leaps still encounter resistance in Britain and Europe. Sadly, the negative characterisation of Muslims in popular discourse (whether political or journalistic) have frozen 'them' as outside of the norm, hence suitable for exclusive and discriminatory action by the mainstream. I hope this book will make some positive contribution in bridging that gap between understanding and action.

Murtaza Shibli

July 2010

7/7 & Me

Mohammed Amin

Mohammed Amin retired as a Tax Partner in PricewaterhouseCoopers to concentrate full time on his voluntary sector activities, all of which focus on the integration of Muslims within British society. In this regard, he has a number of roles, including being a member of the Central Working Committee of the Muslim Council of Britain (MCB) and chairman of the MCB's Business & Economics Committee, Vice-Chairman of the Conservative Muslim Forum, Treasurer of the Muslim Jewish Forum of Greater Manchester, serving on the advisory panel of Good Business Practice, (a charity which promotes better ethical standards in business life) and being a member of the advisory council of the Three Faiths Forum. He is writing in a personal capacity and his views should not be attributed to any organisation.

WHEN I was asked what 7 July 2005 means to me, my first reaction was to step back and ask myself the question "Who am I?"

I was born in Pakistan but have lived in Manchester since I was less than two years old. I have no memories of Pakistan and have never set foot there since my migration. When President Bhutto pulled Pakistan out of the Commonwealth, I chose to become a British citizen rather than having my status in Britain change to 'alien'. However, somewhere in my personal files I still have an expired Pakistani passport (never used for actual travel anywhere) which I obtained when I was about 18, and I have never found any reason to renounce my Pakistani citizenship. By religion I am a Muslim and professionally a chartered accountant and a chartered tax adviser. On 7/7 I was a tax partner based at the Manchester office of PricewaterhouseCoopers but made regular business trips to London.

The day before, 6 July 2005, was a memorable day in its own right. That was the day that London was awarded the right to host the 2012 Olympic Games following outstanding lobbying by the British Olympic bid organising team aided by Prime Minister Tony Blair. I personally felt a massive sense of exultation at getting the Olympics, which was shared by most of the country. Sadly the excitement was to be shattered the following day.

On Thursday 7 July, I was working in my office in Manchester. After wandering around the building to see another tax partner, I was casually chatting with his secretary. She mentioned a mutual colleague who at times is somewhat accident prone! He was down in London and the secretary mentioned with some levity that our accident prone colleague had been unable to get to his meeting due to a power failure on the Underground!

Over the next hour or so the news gradually emerged that there had been a bomb and that some people had been killed. Then gradually the full enormity of the attacks emerged. My wife's family are from the London area and many of them work in central London, some near the area of the bombings. My elder daughter was a student at University College London. Accordingly for several hours my wife and my brothers and sisters in law were making frantic telephone calls to make contact with and account for all of our relatives. The task was made harder as the mobile phone system was jammed by hundreds of thousands of other people trying to do the same thing. Fortunately nobody in our family was injured or killed. However as I write this, tears fill my eyes thinking about the many other people who were similarly trying to call their loved ones only to be met initially by silence, followed by the dreadful horror of learning that their relatives and friends had been seriously injured or killed.

Our standard office hours ended at 1730 but I almost always worked later than that. However I had full discretion when I wanted to come and go, especially as I was a partner in the firm. I recall that I did not rush home from work immediately but worked quite late before going home to face the 24-hour television news channels. Exactly the same thing had happened on 11 September 2001, when by early evening the office was deserted but I was still working; subconsciously I preferred the comfortable environment of the office rather than watching the continuous horror on the television. I knew that once I got home I would be glued to the television screen.

My next memory is of the following Monday, 11 July, when I was due to attend an all-day PricewaterhouseCoopers training event in London. As always, I took the train from Manchester to London Euston. At London Euston the taxi queue seemed to be a mile long, stretching all the way back into the main station concourse, far longer than I have ever seen it. That didn't matter to me as I was already determined to take the Underground. My attitude was the very simple British one "I'll be damned before I let those bastards frighten me away from continuing my normal life by taking the Underground." Despite this being the rush hour, the underground train was pretty empty, although not completely deserted. Obviously, many regular passengers had decided to avoid the risk of underground travel, evidenced also by the length of the taxi queue. I got to the training event on time. About an hour and a half later another partner from Manchester arrived, very late, despite having travelled from Manchester on time. He explained that his wife had only allowed him to attend the London training event on the express promise that he would not use the Underground; he had given up on the taxi queue and had walked all the way from Euston to the hotel where the training event was taking place.

The evening of the following day, 12 July, was bright and sunny and I was in Heaton Park in Manchester, the largest municipal park in the city. I was attending an event called 'Saudi Arabian Days' organised by the Saudi Embassy to showcase Saudi business and culture. It was a glittering occasion with no effort spared, including transporting camels to Manchester. At the event I had a long conversation with a Muslim member of the House of Lords and other leading members of the Muslim community. I think that very day the identity of the suicide bombers had finally been established and it was clear that they were not terrorists sent from abroad but home-grown British Muslims who wished to kill their countrymen. All of us recognised how terrible this was and the potential for a backlash against the British Muslim community.

Enormous praise is due to the Mayor of London at that time, Ken Livingstone, for the way that he pulled Londoners together to prevent the divisions that the killers obviously hoped to foment. Londoners of all religions came together to recognise their common humanity and great credit is due to Ken and to our national politicians of all parties who recognised the need for Britons to unite.

There is a saying that history repeats itself, the first time as tragedy and then as farce. Two weeks later on Thursday 21 July I was driving between meetings in Bradford and Blackburn. I stopped at the motorway services for lunch and as I did so was listening to the BBC Radio 4 news at 1300. This reported the failed bombings in London that day. While greatly relieved that nobody had been hurt, I had to smile at the ineptness of this particular gang of terrorists. Sadly the following day tragedy struck again with the catastrophe of the mistaken killing by the police of Jean Charles de Menezes.

Since then, there have been many other terrorist plots by Muslims. Fortunately, all have been successfully prevented by our security services, or like the attack on Glasgow airport, have failed. The consequences for the British Muslim community if these attacks had succeeded would have been terrible, as we would have seen an anti-Muslim backlash. Sadly that is one of the key goals of these terrorists, to divide British Muslims from other British citizens, and to cause us to tear our country apart, the way that some other countries have been nearly destroyed by internal strife. I do not want to see British Muslims being interned like the Japanese residents of the United States during World War II or being expelled. However nothing would please the terrorists more.

Stepping back and reflecting over the last five years, the following points come to mind. Some Muslims are in complete denial. They simply do not accept that the 7/7 bombings were carried out by Muslims. Instead they believe in conspiracy theories such as pinning the blame on the British government (to provide an excuse for government anti-Muslim policies) or pinning the blame on outfits like Mossad (since Mossad would like to blacken the image of Muslims). Sadly, people are always ready to believe in conspiracies. They never go through the logical thought process of asking how many people inside the British security services and government would need to know about an official government plot to murder its own citizens, and the likelihood that every one of these people would remain silent.

Another sector of the community accept that the bombings were carried out by the individuals named, Mohammad Sidique Khan and others, but somehow don't regard them as Muslims. It is true that setting off bombs on the Underground is a very un-Islamic thing to do. However, if you had been able to observe the lifestyle of these individuals prior to 7 July 2005 you would have seen them reading the Qur'an regularly, praying regularly, fasting and doing everything else that you see Muslims do. Accordingly, in my view you have to accept that these people were Muslims by any objective measure. This applies even if your view theologically is that once they formed the intention to commit mass murder they had distanced themselves from God and turned away from everything that Islam stands for.

The most common thing I hear from the Muslim community is that the bombers did it because of our country's foreign policy, especially Britain's unbalanced support for Israel and our country's invasion of Iraq, which almost all British citizens now recognise to have been utterly misconceived. It is clearly true that those were the reasons why these people chose to kill, since they have told us that in their suicide videos. However, stopping the analysis at that point is seriously incomplete. There are hundreds of thousands if not millions of Britons who feel equally strongly about issues such as Palestine and Iraq who do not become suicide bombers. Almost all of the British Muslim community feels strongly about Palestine and Iraq but apart from a tiny minority of terrorists, British Muslims confine themselves to lawful opposition and political protest. What was different about the bombers?

Looking at the suicide videos, the bombers clearly believed that the bombings they were about to carry out would be a good deed in the eyes of God. It is clear to me that these individuals did not expect to go to hell as a consequence of their actions but instead expected to go to heaven. If they had believed that they were going to hell, they would not have carried out their actions. Many brave people are willing to give up their lives for their religious beliefs in order to serve God with the hope of entering paradise. However I cannot conceive of anyone who is religious wanting to promote a political cause on earth, if this means consciously defying God and consciously choosing to be cast into hell for all eternity.

I have laboured this point because many in the British Muslim community deny that the religious beliefs of the killers matter. I suspect that the people with this position think that if they accept that the killers were influenced by their religious beliefs, somehow this will reflect badly on Islam. Such a view is completely wrong; God's true religion cannot be tarnished by the crimes committed by a few (or even by many) Muslims. Islam's truth cannot be tainted by human misconduct.

However, while there is no problem with Islam, there is a problem with some Muslims which we need to face up to. While I believe that if I were to kill a random collection of Londoners God would sentence me to hell for all eternity, there are some Muslims who think that such conduct would be a passport to heaven. Such people are dangerous because once they believe that God has given them permission to kill British citizens they will try to do it unless our country subordinates its policies to their view of the world. Today it is our foreign policy in any one of a number of places; tomorrow it will be our country's policy of allowing people to drink alcohol or to wear miniskirts.

What we need is a clear and consistent message from all Muslim leaders, repeated regularly, that killing other people – except in self-defence or in a legally declared war – is a crime against the law of God which will result in you being sent to hell. Only when this is accepted by all British Muslims will we be free from the threat of terrorist acts being committed by misguided Muslims.

As citizens, we also face dangers from other would-be terrorists such as homophobes, anti-Muslim bigots, Irish republicans and others. However, as I was asked to reflect upon 7/7, I have focused on the danger from those Muslims who are seriously misguided about Islam.

I occasionally think about how I might feel after discovering that one of my sons or daughters had become a terrorist. Apart from the shock, I think the overwhelming reaction would be one of guilt, to ask "Where did I go wrong; what did I fail to teach him or her?" Fortunately, my own children have been brought up in an atmosphere where they were encouraged to think independently, and show no signs of religious extremism. Nor have they encountered the problems I hear about from other Muslims such as repeated stop and search which can cause people to become less supportive of the police. The key vaccines against becoming a religiously motivated terrorist are a true understanding of one's religion and real appreciation for our society and the way that it governs itself.

Making the Connection

Laura Stout

Laura Stout is currently a Masters student at Birkbeck University, studying Nationalism and Ethnic Conflict, having graduated with a degree in Anthropology from University College London (UCL) in 2006. While studying, she also works at the Muslim Council of Britain (MCB) as PA to the Secretary General. Having only reverted in 2008, Laura enjoys spending as much time as possible learning about Islam and the diverse Muslim community. She is aware this is a long journey on which she is just embarking on and hopes to make a positive contribution – inshaAllah (God willing). Laura is married and lives in London.

IT'S strange how you can often remember exactly where you were at crucial moments of history. I can remember precisely what I was doing on the 11th of September 2001 and later on the 7th of July 2005, when terrorist attacks sent New York and London respectively into panic.

In 2001 I was 18 and had just embarked on my gap year. I was working full-time as a cashier in our local supermarket while I saved up to go travelling that December. On the day the hijacked planes plummeted into the twin towers, I was serving the customers and a number of them started to report back to me what they had seen on the TVs in our electrical aisle. It wasn't long before I had to go and look for myself and I remember being very confused and shocked that a seemingly untouchable America had been so noticeably and substantially hurt. As a teenage, agnostic, English girl, I interestingly don't recall making the connection between the attacks and Islam – although this may have been because my awareness and interest in politics was shamefully negligible at the time. I can remember feeling worried that the UK would be next, but when after a few days had passed and this hadn't happened and the news coverage of the dramatic event increasingly reduced, the fear gradually faded. Life just went back to normal – for me anyway.

In July of 2005, I awoke in my student flat in central London to find several missed calls from my mum on my mobile. Upon realising my phone would not connect to call her back, I became aware of the helicopters circling the area over my flat and I switched on my TV to see if that would bring any clarification. The channels were all covering the same thing – news of the explosions on the Underground. Panic set in. I was living near Warren Street at the time and so I wasn't that far away from Kings Cross, where one of the attacks had taken place. My main concern was that I couldn't call anyone to tell them I was okay and I couldn't check to see if my friends had been affected. I quickly grabbed a bag of essentials – not knowing when I'd next come back to the flat – and made my way out. The streets were swarming, which served to panic me even more! Everyone seemed to be trying to walk out of London! Although it was now nearly 10am, there was eerily hardly any traffic. I followed the crowd, winding down the streets towards Camden until I found a small internet cafe. Soon I was connected and I was able to tell my family I was safe. Slowly, one by one, I discovered my friends were accounted for. Once I knew everyone was safe, I decided the best thing to do was to carry on walking out of town in case another attack happened. Even when I was safely inside my friends' house a couple of hours later I could not relax – the television showed the same harrowing pictures again and again. It was the number of attacks I think that caused most concern and the fact one had taken place on a bus. The quantity and variety made me wonder where and who would be next and where it was safest to be.

In the aftermath, security was tight and I was very conscious of not looking suspicious around the high alert police officers that seemed to be out in full force in the days afterwards. It was with disbelief I learnt that the men who had caused this devastation, less than a mile away from where I lived, were British born. Everyone was walking on egg shells – I guess that's the nature of an attack from 'the inside': everyone looks like they could be up to no good and no stranger can be trusted. I was as bad as everyone else I'm ashamed to say – I can remember avoiding travelling on the tube for a few months after the explosions took place. I would go to extraordinary lengths to do so – taking numerous buses to my destination. Also, if an Asian man with a beard got on the tube with a rucksack I would find my heart beating faster and I wouldn't be able to relax until myself or he left the train. In hindsight this sounds stupid but I guess it's a natural, survival instinct and Asian men with beards were a visible target for my fear, despite my rational mind telling me otherwise!

Saying that, I can honestly say I still don't remember making the connection between any of these attacks and Islam as a religion! Religion to me has always been a positive force rather than a negative and I couldn't imagine a religion that would encourage people to blow themselves up in the middle of crowded public spaces! I have always been very reluctant to put people into boxes and label groups of people with attributes – good or bad. I really don't understand how people cannot look outside the box and question if stereotypes are really true for everyone that happens to fall into that category! The same was true of 9/11 and 7/7. I think you really need to look at why these individuals did what they did rather than just making sweeping general statements that inevitably breed misunderstanding, increased ignorance, fear and hate. Seeking to understand the root causes just seems like common sense – although I appreciate it is not an easy task.

A Different Understanding

My reversion to Islam, in April 2008, had nothing to do with what happened in New York or London. When I was introduced to Islam, it was through a Muslim friend and then through a book by a non-Muslim author about Prophet Muhammad (prayers and peace be upon him). When people ask why I decided, at 24 years old, to completely and so dramatically change my life, I feel they can be somewhat disappointed with my response! It was not a near death experience, it was not a bolt of lightning, it wasn't even because I fell in love with a Muslim man (as some would expect!) – It simply made sense and I followed my head and my heart in making the decision. I had struggled with my faith and where I stood on the topic of God for years. I felt Christianity didn't have the answers to the questions I had. Islam? Well it just made sense.

My understanding of Islam is a million miles away from the pictures I hear and see painted around me. It is a religion that encourages love, forgiveness and compassion for the world and those around us. It teaches us to live together side by side in peace, regardless of religion, colour, nationality, class and culture. It speaks of a deeply held respect for women, family values and equality – with an appreciation for the different attributes we've all been given, and giving charity to the poor, orphaned, widowed and destitute. It provides guidance on how to become a better version of who you are, how to build and strengthen a relationship with our Creator who is so loving, most forgiving and just, and how to make a positive contribution during our short time on this earth.

So when I reverted and people started to ask me what I thought of the suicide bombers you can imagine that the questions felt quite bizarre and so far removed from what I had, day by day, fallen in love with. At the time, I actually laughed off their comments but, in hindsight, these people were just looking for reassurance. I had reverted to a religion to which they held negative connotations and it wasn't long until I started to see why they held these views.

Interestingly, the negative, destructive images and stories of Muslims and Islam that I became aware of did not come from the community but from the outside world. Some days I would catch myself actually rolling my eyes at the articles in the paper I was reading. It seemed to me that any negative story that happened to involve a Muslim included a description of his religion. Everyone else was described by their gender, age, even colour – but you never heard of a Christian or atheist fraudster! It was this sense of unequal treatment which upset me and it angered me that a lot of people reading the paper wouldn't even be aware of this bias and would just accept it as objective fact. I know being a Muslim does not make you perfect and a lot of people who say they follow a certain religion do not match their actions with their words, but the emphasis and negativity towards Islam was apparent and disproportionate. Stereotypes – however exaggerated and generalist – often have a basis of truth. It was my journey of understanding the basis of truth which at times left me somewhat disillusioned with the Muslim community but always strengthened my faith and trust in Allah.

JIHAD

Jihad is a word that has, in my opinion, been used to scare people about Islam. It is a foreign word, wrapped in mystery and people are scared of what they don't know. I really think it's about time we explained it to everyone clearly and attempted to de-mystify it. Jihad, in my own words, means 'striving for good' and overcoming obstacles in the process. This can be anything from striving to gain a qualification to striving to feed the homeless. It basically applies to anything good anyone strives for despite enduring difficulties. Jihad can mean fighting but only in self-defence – be that individually or for your country.

I have had my own personal jihad since becoming Muslim. We are taught in the Qur'an that we should expect to be tested and I definitely know this to be the case. Being a Muslim is a constant test of character and faith. Circumstances and situations occur which mean you can act in a way which is in accordance with your faith or not. It is choosing to stand up for what you think is right, the courage to continue with your vision of who you are, who you want to be and what is important to you. It can mean not being popular with those around you, along with despair and deep questioning of the self, others and the truth. Jihad is facing these difficulties, being self critical of your intentions and your actions, and pursuing your actions if you still believe them to be right.

I would like to state clearly now that I do not support what those men did when they attacked New York and London, but I do believe it is important to understand why they did what they did, without attempting to justify their actions. There is never a simple answer to why people find themselves in these positions – a number of factors are often at play. However, in my humble, fairly ignorant opinion they were most probably manipulated, by people who were politically motivated or had something to gain from their actions, into thinking that their actions would be seen as striving against injustice and therefore as acts of jihad. As mentioned above, jihad can be about striving against injustice; however it also requires actions to be in line with other key principles of Islam – including patience, peace and wanting for others what you want for yourself. Islam is a religion that values life not its destruction.

But why were these individuals so readily convinced? I do think a lack of clear leadership within the community is one of the factors involved. It is a difficult situation as the Muslim community is very diverse – in terms of culture, origin and approach – and Islam does not have a clear hierarchical leadership structure that other religions have – for example, Catholicism. While equality of all men and women before Allah is something that really appeals to me about Islam, it certainly can raise questions about who to trust as leaders or scholars. As a new Muslim, it was and still is quite overwhelming and confusing to work out who to listen to or which speakers to trust. I have been at lectures or gatherings where I have felt quite uncomfortable with what the speakers have been saying. One vital lesson I learnt soon after I reverted is to rely on no-one but Allah to guide you and to always check out for yourself what people are quoting. Quotes from the Qur'an can be taken out of context and translations can lead to certain sentences meaning something completely different. I have learnt to cross-reference my Qur'an translations and to ask a variety of people on their understanding of certain verses in order to grasp a well rounded definition. Hadith (sayings or actions of Prophet Muhammad, prayers and peace be upon him) also need to be checked for authenticity and again need to be taken in the context of the greater meaning of Islam. Allah has given us brains so we can question and explore for ourselves the world around us and the teachings of our religion. However, because this takes a lot more effort than relying on other people for answers and because of the sheer volume of scholarly work, the complexities of the Arabic language and the amount of cross referencing involved – I can understand why a lot of people do choose to blindly trust others. However, if the person you place trust in is not worthy or is, in fact, misguided – this can have disastrous effects. If the ideology behind 9/11 and 7/7 was closely scrutinised by those taking part, they would have seen that Islam would not teach this. The attacks were direct attacks, targeted mainly at civilians – something completely opposed to the true understanding of jihad. It is my understanding that Allah has defined our limits in the Qur'an and anything in excess which breaches those limits, comes from us and is questionable.

LASTING IMPACT

Since my reversion, the events of 9/11 and 7/7 have had a big impact on my life in a number of ways. The negative views of Islam and Muslims in general have become more vocalised and popular, as has the national rise of the British National Party (BNP). It is now me who can be the object of suspicion when I get on the tube with a rucksack and headscarf! I can imagine what other people may be thinking – it wasn't long ago that I was sat in their seats, thinking the same thing! They cannot help being scared. However, I am certain there are things on both sides of the train carriage – Muslim and non-Muslim – that could be done to improve community cohesion and relations while also reducing the risk of these attacks happening again. I have mentioned a few things here but would like to make clear that these are things I remind myself of as much as anyone else.

First of all, everyone needs to recognise and accept that prejudice and discrimination are things we could all readily do without, and that effort is required to eradicate these things from our world. They are based on ignorance and the only way to combat them is through education. This is two way and applies to Muslims and non-Muslims alike and while this may appear as stating the obvious, unfortunately it seems it still needs to be said!

Non-Muslims need to be encouraged to be more critical of what they read about Islam and Muslims, and be more aware of the fact that nothing is objective. Some already do this but unfortunately not enough people! In order to critique Islam you need to research it and you need to do this with an open mind, searching for the truth of the teachings rather than just believing what you read in the papers to be objective fact. Unless you do this, you will interpret things the way your pre-conceptions encourage you to. If Muslims are saying that Islam is a religion of peace and you think that it is backward, chauvinistic and violent – then perhaps it is worth stepping into a Muslim's shoes and trying to understand the situation from our side of the carriage. Muslims are rational human beings too – there are reasons why we think, believe and value the things we do. You don't need to agree but it would help if we all attempted to understand each other's differences.

Muslims must be careful not to stereotype non-Muslims in a similar way. Yes there are things about Western culture in general that Islam does not agree with, for example, drinking alcohol, but Muslims must remember that it is our Islamic duty to respect that other people believe differently to us. The fact we differ on these issues of what is right and wrong is established – we now have to see past these differences and work together. We must celebrate the positive things about the country we live in – the freedom to practice our religion, women's rights, the right to vote, free schooling and healthcare for all citizens. We should be addressing together the problems of this world – climate change, the number of homeless people on our streets in the depths of winter, the inequality and poverty we see both at home and abroad, child labour and other forms of exploitation, child abuse, forced marriages, domestic violence and the list, unfortunately and all too well known, goes on. This is where our focus should be! Not on internal squabbles! The challenge before us is huge and we must unite if we stand a chance.

As Muslims we also need to understand that one of the reasons why others have a negative view of us and Islam is that we often don't practice what we preach. On this point I would go back to non-Muslims and urge them not to judge Islam by how we practice it! Muslims are not perfect either and fall short as much as anyone. This happens on an individual and national level. As I have mentioned above, as a revert I have at times felt very disillusioned with the Muslim community. It took a while for me to realise that I too was guilty of putting all Muslims in a box. A box which meant I'd labelled them all as trustworthy, honest people who would always stand up for what was right. But people are people. Someone once told me that we have to treat humans as humans, not angels: that is to say we are not perfect. That has stayed with me and has helped me at times of injustice, frustration and disappointment. However, Muslims need to understand that the work must begin internally.

Firstly, education about Islam, both within and outside the Muslim community, needs to be increased and made clearer. The teachings of justice, equality, unity, fairness etc. must be focussed on, instead of the teaching concentrating only on the ritual and legal aspects of Islam. In the same way, the 'khutba' during Friday prayers needs to focus more on what Islam teaches regarding how we treat each other! We need to wake up and realise we are letting ourselves and society down by not allowing these teachings to penetrate the very essence of who we are. This includes behaving in a way that reflects Islam when expressing our views. For example, in order to resist insults and fight Islamophobia we must act in a way which does Islam justice! We cannot scream and shout! We have to abide by the law and the system in this country if we want to be a part of it and make a difference. And the only way to bring about positive change is from within. We must fight the pen with the pen, we must engage and debate and, above all, we must contribute! We must get ourselves down to the polling stations – now more than ever before! We must speak up and speak out against injustice – and not just that which affects the Muslim community – all injustice! We must not segregate ourselves – we should make every attempt to correct ourselves with the guidance of Islam and then let our characters teach others what Islam is truly about. Without making these changes within ourselves, how can we expect people to see Islam for the positive influence it can truly be?

Secondly, we must invest in our young people. Young Muslims are struggling with the normal youth related issues such as bullying, image and fitting in, but also with issues such as Islamophobia and a greater generational gap between themselves and their parents, who often struggle to understand the culture and issues their children are experiencing. Generally, the Muslim community is disproportionately poorer than the rest of society and therefore the youth are often facing issues such as the overcrowding of living space, gang culture and resisting the temptation to gain access to illegal sources of income in order to wear the latest fashion and drive the best cars etc. This can unfortunately lead to additional problems like drugs and prostitution. While this makes very uncomfortable reading, it is sadly the reality and we must not hide from it but face it head on. Thankfully we have a number of organisations and individuals that are providing services for our young people but are we doing enough?

The stereotypes that have blossomed as a result of 9/11 and 7/7 have left more of a lasting impression on me than I first realised. It has left me determined to be a part of the solution and I believe Islam's teachings of peace, education, respect, patience and gratefulness (among others) can, if really put into practice, help make stronger connections and build bridges between people. The challenge is huge but you either chose to make a relatively small contribution or you become a passive bystander. I choose to get involved.

LONG NIGHT, LONGER DAY

RUHUL TARAFDER

Ruhul Tarafder is the Communications Manager with IF charity based in East London. Previously he has worked on various national campaigns for Muslims including anti-racism and human rights. He has been on the management committee of the Youth Action Scheme, a primarily Bangladeshi Muslim youth project based in Tower Hamlets. One of the highlights of this was to take several football teams over to Denmark each year to participate in the Dana Cup, the second largest youth football tournament in the world. He has also participated in conflict resolution and mediation work between gangs in London.

IT was a long night on July 6th 2005. Shahed and I had been in Scotland for the last few days attending the protests against the G8 summit. It was there that representatives of the world's great powers were attending their annual gathering to discuss issues including world trade and climate change. At the time I was working for the 1990 Trust, the first UK national black organisation set up to protect and pioneer the interest of Britain's black communities ('Black' was a political term referring to all people of African, Caribbean and Asian descent). I had requested my boss, Karen Chouhan, if we could go to Scotland to join the protests. Even though the Trust was part of the 'Make Poverty History' campaign, we felt that for a number of reasons there was very little visible 'black' involvement in the movement so we should attend.

The week began with the Make Poverty History rally in Edinburgh on Saturday. Over 200,000 people from charities, unions and faith groups had come together to call upon Tony Blair and other world leaders to deliver trade justice, debt cancellation and better aid for the world's poorest countries.

Over the next few days I witnessed running battles between police officers and protesters in the heart of Edinburgh city centre as well as a near enough full scale riot at the perimeter fence near Auchterarder where the world leaders were meeting. The climax of this was when the police were flown in on helicopters in a military style operation above our heads. The next thing we knew we were running through fields of wheat to escape police, marauding dogs and their handlers who were giving chase.

That seemed to be enough excitement for one week so we decided that since we were already in Scotland, and had a hired car to hand, why not explore the land of bagpipes and Braveheart? Whilst in Edinburgh, we met with a close friend of ours, Shamiul, and invited him to join us but he insisted he couldn't do so as he had to return to London for work purposes. We listened attentively, said we would drop him off at the station and then headed straight for John O' Groats.

Over the next couple of days we witnessed the spectacular beauty of the region staying in the capital of the highlands, Inverness, before driving to Fort William alongside the shoreline of the stunning Loch Ness. The breathtaking beauty of Scotland left shimmering impressions on our hearts only to be shattered by the events awaiting us in a few hours time.

We considered staying in Scotland for a few more days but as Shamiul was now insisting that he would be sacked if we didn't return to London by tomorrow (July 7th), we resolved to drive through the night back to London. We contemplated which route to take back, and decided that instead of the safe and simple route of the motorway we had come by, there was an alternative route through deep forests and country roads. We decided on the latter but soon discovered that as it was now pitch black there was very little that we could actually see apart from dense forest and the occasional glimpse of the moon. In fact, it seemed like we were the only people using this road. We were all contemplating whether the AA covered these kinds of remote areas in the event of a breakdown. If they did, we had no idea of how we were to give a location description, anyway!

The smugness of knowing we had a hired car soon took over my driving behaviour. I felt I was in a world rally championship and thoroughly enjoyed driving up and down steep hills and through the dense forests in the middle of the night, at the same time trying to spot a sign directing us towards London. The experience was the encouragement needed for myself and Shahed to drive from Banglatown to Bangladesh a few years later.

Shahed and I took it in turns from here to drive towards London. As daylight broke we approached the city of London, our home! Shahed drove to his house in White City. I took over the driving from this point and dropped off Shamiul somewhere near Paddington station at around 8.00am. From here I headed east towards my flat in Aldgate, extremely tired but trying to beat the worst of the morning rush hour. I was listening to the radio when at around 9.00am the news reported an incident between Liverpool Street and Aldgate. I had driven through Marylebone Road and passed Kings Cross, just longing to reach my bed now when reports on the radio talked of more explosions caused by a power surge. I remember thinking, "power surge, yeah right". Of course I would rather it be that than some kind of terrorist attack, even though the loss of life in either case would be a tragedy. But deep down I knew it wasn't.

Every day I would hear on the radio or read in the papers about the radicalisation of Muslims. The government would blame the mosques and the imams and suggest that the problem was inherent within the Muslim community and that we needed to do something about it, but I knew it wasn't that at all. Yes, people were becoming more radical. I had seen and been involved with the anti-war movement myself, and observed how from the earlier rallies at Trafalgar Square, where there had been a handful of Muslims, as the war drew closer, these handfuls had turned into tens of thousands. We had all become radical, and I was one of them, but whereas the vast majority of people were angry but completely peaceful, it only needed a few psycho individuals to take things to another level and do some crazy shit.

The irony was that, contrary to the government spin blaming the community and institutions, I had become radicalised simply by watching Sky News, BBC and Channel 4. The daily cocktail of pictures and stories from Iraq accompanied by the hypocrisy and double standards of US and UK foreign policy was what was doing the radicalising. Of course this was in no way a justification of any kind for committing acts of terror but it was an explanation. How long were we going to keep brushing things under the carpet and not look at the real root causes, as uncomfortable as they may seem? So I wondered, was it as Malcolm X had once said when Kennedy was assassinated, "The chickens coming home to roost?" I hoped not.

The traffic now seemed to be getting worse by the minute, so I decided to take several back streets before finally arriving home completely drained and exhausted. On entering my flat, I turned on the TV, and lay down on my bed. I thought to myself, let me just see what was happening in the city. By now there were more explosions, the Underground system was being shut down and I was just waiting for them to confirm it was a terror attack. From my window I could hear more and more police sirens, fire engines and ambulances driving past my flat, towards Aldgate Station. I lived less than half a mile from the station and the famous Brick Lane and was thinking, "Wow, that's quite close."

I tried using my phone. There seemed to be no network and I think at that stage the tiredness got the better of me and I dozed off. It must have been at least an hour or two before I awoke with TV presenters now talking of co-ordinated terrorist attacks across London including Edgware Road and Kings Cross. An explosion had taken place on a bus too in Tavistock Square, all of which had resulted in many deaths and injuries. I prayed that no-one I knew would be on any of the trains or the bus and felt appalled at what I was seeing.

As I watched events unfold, I was contemplating again, who would do this? Was it an attack aimed at destroying the summit we had just left in Scotland? Could it have been something to do with the anarchist groups who were protesting, sometimes violently in Edinburgh? Or was it more likely to be something related to the war in Iraq. Were the attackers Muslim in origin? Somehow I felt it was the latter.

I was thinking, if this is the work of terrorists and they came from a Muslim background, there would be a backlash against Muslims who would be blamed as a community for this. The government and in particular Tony Blair was constantly trying to deny a link between foreign policy, and the growth in radicalism as a consequence. Would people understand this or simply blame all Muslims? On awakening once again several hours later, I realised the hire car was now overdue. Maybe they would take into account today's events but, then again, probably not.

I imagined that my work load at the Trust would greatly increase over the subsequent, weeks and months. My role there had evolved into one of working on issues such as the increase in Islamophobia and racist attacks upon Muslims. If these explosions on the Underground were attacks by terrorists who were

Muslim, it would certainly result in an increase in verbal and physical attacks upon the community too. Over the next few days details emerged about who was responsible and why. Once again, there seemed to be little acknowledgment of the role of foreign policy.

At work I was following reports from around the country of attacks upon the Muslim community. People had been assaulted, spat at and there were reports of women having their hijabs torn off. Muslims tend to be distinctive and I feared for my dad who had a beard and lived in a predominantly white area. After 7/7 someone tried to run him over outside the mosque. An old age pensioner! I really feared for my sisters as some wear a hijab. Some women I know were thinking of not wearing a hijab as the climate after the bombings had become more hostile.

Three days after the 7th July bombings, a 48-year old Pakistani, Kamal Butt, was murdered outside a corner shop in Nottingham. Mosques had been attacked, a garage firebombed, people assaulted in the street, and homes vandalized and sprayed with graffiti. Was this the beginning of something? As well as the attacks in the media, it was as if every morning, Muslims were expected to wake up and issue an apology before starting the day. It was as if they were responsible for the crimes of these four lunatic individuals. I remember wondering at the time why we seemed to be going round in circles. Muslims were not looking for a Muslim friendly foreign policy, but just one that was fair and just. Co-operation and understanding was needed between all communities and the Muslim community needed to be fully accepted and valued as a part of life in Britain.

Of course I was sickened by these mindless acts of violence, which had claimed so many lives and destroyed so many dreams and visions. However, I also stopped to think on that day what the consequences could be for our community and around the world. Everything could change just like it did after 9/11. Would there be more attacks such as those on Afghanistan where more bombs would be dropped from planes from miles above on the pretext of hunting Bin Laden? I now felt very conscious after the bombings every time I set foot outside. Was it me being paranoid? After the tragic death of Jean Charles de Menezes, who was shot several times after being mistaken for a terrorist, I knew the world and my world had changed. Since then I have seen many friends questioned by police and have suffered this same fate myself for several hours on a flight back from Prague.

As the weeks passed, there were many commentators who realised that the actions of a few people did not represent a whole religion and who were encouraging the need for deeper understanding and dialogue between faiths and communities. Others seemed to want to promote division and intolerance. Did the nutcases committing these atrocities ever think of the consequences of their actions? Not only upon the immediate victims but also upon the community in whose name they were committing these acts of terror; the elderly woman living in Somerset, the young hijabi in North Wales or the bearded uncle in Essex.

But for me, until the killings in Iraq and Palestine and Afghanistan stopped, whilst we were setting fire to other peoples countries, whilst we were killing other people's mothers and fathers, brothers and sisters, whilst we were occupying other peoples lands, there would always be a possibility of anger, resentment, resistance and revenge in the minds of some, however abhorrent attacks on innocent civilians were. We conduct war through our modern machinery. They conduct terror through their bombings. Are they not one and the same thing? As I once read, "War is the terrorism of the rich and powerful and terrorism is the war of the poor and powerless."

Again, this is in no way a justification, just an explanation.

Unpacking Suitcases
British Muslim Identity
Before and After 7/7

Sadia Habib

Sadia Habib has taught at 6th form level in Bury, Lancashire, and at secondary school and 6th form in South East London. Her undergraduate studies and PGCE training were completed at the University of Leicester. She obtained her MA in Education at Goldsmiths, University of London where she developed her interest in issues of identity, diaspora, masculinities and femininities, multilingualism and literacy, children's literature and diversity. In her spare time, she enjoys writing theatre reviews for Manchester Mouth (an online minority news and community affairs site). Currently, she is working towards her doctorate in Educational Studies at Goldsmiths College.

WITH the anniversary of the atrocities of 7/7 approaching, my thoughts are on the journey of Muslims in Britain, from the once, perhaps, temporary nature of our belonging in Britain to the permanent roots we have now established here. Young British Muslims, today, know that we are here to stay: we belong to Britain and Britain belongs to us. Surely we must keep discussing and defining, re-examining and re-exploring the shifting nature of identities such as British Muslim.

BECOMING BRITISH

The horrific events of 7/7 brought the question of British Muslim identity into the limelight. My parents' generation felt alienated from this new generation of youth who seemed to be expressing a type of 'dis-integration' in British society. They clearly could not fathom, like many of us, how 7/7 could have happened. Young British Muslim boys committing suicide supposedly for 'religious' causes was beyond the comprehension of my parents and their generation. The older generation felt disconnected from the 'mindless'[1] mentality of these boys. They became anxious about the socio-political ramifications of 7/7: the potential for

---

1 I use the term 'mindless' because although the 7/7 suicide bombers could be seen as calculating, still, their actions were mindless.

backlash against Muslims, moral panic created by the media and an increased support for the British National Party (BNP). They felt uneasy about their position in a place they called home. The tragic events of 7/7 re-ignited my interest in identity issues. I began to recall how my parents and their friends struggled with notions of home and belonging in their time.

Living in Lancashire, my parents and their friends talking over dinner forever planning the 'Immigrant's Dream'. One day they would permanently return to their homeland of Pakistan. They witnessed friends building a 'home' in Pakistan for holidays, for retirement, or in case events in Idi Amin's Uganda were repeated here. It is etched in my memory that my parents and their friends kept their clothes in their suitcases. There were clothes in their wardrobes, too, but for some reason, they never fully unpacked their suitcases. My sister and I would stumble across these suitcases in my parents' bedroom or at the homes of family friends and wonder at the temporary nature of our being in Britain.

To some young people today, it may be unbelievable that you can be 'evicted' from your own country – but for my parents' generation it was a real fear, especially considering they had heard political discourse such as Enoch Powell's infamous "Rivers of Blood" speech and Norman Tebbit's "cricket test". They had seen what had happened in Southall when the National Front clashed with those who lived there. Racism was the norm. They had come to Britain for a better life, but belonging in Britain, being British and becoming British were not easy or straightforward identifications. Their Britain was not necessarily a welcoming place; a cold climate and even colder attitudes meant that my parents' generation knew their 'place' and it wasn't Britain. Thus, for a while, they maintained a solid connection with their homeland in their minds, where they had come from, was home.

Conversations about returning to the homeland (so we could connect with the cultural, linguistic and religious heritage) were to us mere dreams. As the second-generation, we were able to see diasporic discussions and diversions in action. We were living diaspora. We were beginning to understand the complexities of the notions of home and belonging. One day, these conversations of leaving Britain stopped. My parents and their friends seemed to be reluctantly accepting that their notions of home, which once upon a time had been very clear-cut, were now more complex than they had ever thought possible. Their loyalties to Pakistan (the 'mother' country they had long left behind) were now confused with their loyalties for Britain (where they had spent most of their lives).

This idea of a temporary life in Britain, of leaving Britain, of returning to the homeland was a very common migrant experience. The sociologist Stuart Hall (2000) refers to this as an illusion that many first generation immigrants, including he, himself, had. He wonders whether this was because he was always asked about when he was going back home. It is still the case that this concept of 'back home' exists. In my experience, successive second generation, third, fourth and even fifth generations who are settled and feel that Britain is very much their home will still be asked about back home: what is life like back home? How often do you go back home? Where is back home? Sometimes, deliberately, but not awkwardly, when I am asked about where back home is for me, I will reply Lancashire, to challenge assumptions that I call some foreign 'exotic' land 'home' perhaps because of the colour of my skin.

My parents have recognised that their home now is here, in England. I do not think that their desire or dream to return home was merely a myth; in the 1970s and 1980s it was a reality, planned and planned again, thought of as achievable. My parents and their Pakistani friends have gradually, perhaps some might say, even reluctantly, become British.[2]

EVOLVING SOCIETY, EVOLVING SELF

When I was at school, fifteen years ago, I was the only Asian in my year group, and one of very few Asians at the school. I was a novelty; some of my peers were curious about my culture and religion, and some were not curious at all. They all had one thing in common though; they lacked knowledge of Pakistanis or Muslims. One friend in my first year at secondary school was alarmed at the thought of my family not cooking traditional English Christmas dinner, so she kindly insisted that I went to her home on Christmas Day! My peers had no real notion of difference. Or if they did, it was only of negative images of other cultures or religions which stemmed from racist ideologies. A more disturbing incident that I have not forgotten occurred in science class in my first year; a girl, in all seriousness, actually asked me if I used soap.

---

2 Even today, there is an amusing anecdote in my family that when my mum returns to Pakistan – the place where she was born – she suffers with heat spots on her skin. She is English now, we tell her – and she cannot acclimatise herself to Pakistan.

Fifteen years on from my time at school, contemporary Britain seemed a different place. There was more awareness of difference and difference was regarded in a positive light. Such a landscape of modern Britain was a far cry from the place I grew up in. There seemed to be a mutual exchange of values and features between the 'hosts' and the different generations of 'immigrants'. The days of advocating assimilation seemed to be over. Integration seemed to have taken a step forward for the indigenous English were inheriting and being influenced by the values and traditions of those who had settled in their country. My life in Britain and the lives of many religious and ethnic groups seemed stable and successful. That was pre-7/7. And then 7/7 occurred, disrupting notions of home and belonging I think I had become comfortable with.

I was disturbed that this small group of boys should be so socially 'unhinged' that they resort to an act of insanity. I felt ashamed that they supposedly acted in the name of my religion. I know I wasn't alone in feeling distressed about the act itself but also the long-term consequences for Muslims in Britain. I wondered about the impact of 7/7 on social relations between Muslims and other social groups in British society. I was apprehensive about the potential for a 'moral panic' to be portrayed by media organisations.

7/7 damaged our sense of being part of the 'imagined community',[3] raising urgent questions about who belonged, and who felt they did not and why. The atrocious acts raised questions about loyalties to Britain. 7/7 gave me cause to be concerned about the small group of young Muslim males who were involved in this tragedy. As an educationalist, I wanted to learn more about their experience of the school system. As a social researcher, I wanted to know about their experiences of family, work and wider society at large. How had institutions such as the media and polity affected their perspectives of social justice? Why did these boys feel this desperate need to cause such a tragedy? In my view, it is crucial to give these issues due consideration. At the same time, we must always point to how this is a minority mindset. 7/7 was painful for our national psyche, especially so for my parents'

---

3 Benedict Anderson defined nations as being "imagined communities" – "because the members of even the smallest nation will never know most of their fellow-members, meet them, or even hear of them, yet in the minds of each lives the image of their communion...". (Anderson, 2001: 225) Despite some perceptions of the link between nation and "race", I believe that my parents and many of their generation are committed to our "nation", our "imagined community".

generation who are grateful for the opportunities and privileges they have had living here, and would never wish any harm to their adoptive home. The British Muslims I know; my friends and my peers, their friends and peers, condemned these acts of 7/7 as atrocious. My friends and peers are able to be British and be Muslim with ease, for multiple identities is the norm. Diverse identifications are real and lived.

TO BE BRITISH OR NOT TO BE BRITISH?

Disturbing events such as 7/7 call for the urgent need to re-consider notions of home and belonging as situated and discursive. It is crucial that we hear the stories of the younger generations and what they tell us about belonging to Britain. We need to listen to their tales about their place in society and the implications this has on the sense of self. Schools are excellent places to have this very dialogue and debate about whether the young are able to be British and Muslim, and how they manage to perform multiple identities. And of course, we must not forget that the label 'British Muslim' is not homogenous: British Muslims have diverse cultural, linguistic and ethnic identities.

In a post 7/7 Britain, some of us seek a deeper understanding of what it means to be British, what it means to be Muslim, and how such notions of identity can contribute to a harmonious society. Identities are multiple, fluid and shifting: diasporic movement illustrates how a fixed identity bound to a certain village, a certain town, a certain city or a certain nation is no longer the norm. Identities are transforming; continually and constantly being remade, renegotiated, redefined, rediscovered and rewritten by diasporic communities. The passing of time affects how identities are always changing: what Britishness meant to different generations of Pakistanis growing up in the 1970s, the 1980s, and the 1990s will have always been affected by the socio-political climate at the time.

Speaking from multiple identities is possible for British Muslims. We can challenge definitions of Britishness and perceptions of British Muslims that are limiting, excluding or homogenising. To be British and to be Muslim, today, does not have to be mutually exclusive, and what we do – our work, our writings, our social interactions, our relationships and our day-to-day living – manifests this perfectly. From my research with students, and from my experience as a teacher, the young are keen to discuss notions of identity. We need to build on this enthusiasm and give our future generation the space and place to explore where they came from, and who they are today in order that where they are going to be is a place of success and excellence. We need to unpack those ancient battered suitcases of our parents and grandparents – if they have not already been unpacked – and find a place for the 'clothing' we have inherited right next to the British 'clothing' we have acquired on our own terms.[4]

---

4 I could playfully extend this metaphor and refer to our new items of clothing being 'Made in Britain', however it is more than likely these items were 'Made in Pakistan' or Bangladesh, or China.

Under Siege

Raihan Akhtar

Raihan Akhtar is originally from Birmingham and moved to London in 2004 to work as a strategy consultant. He is involved in support and counselling work within the Muslim community.

I HAD been living in London for one and a half years, working at a small management consultancy firm based near Oxford Circus. I have always considered myself to be a deeply spiritual and detached person, and this has always helped me to deal with challenges in my stride. 7th July 2005 was no different.

Since childhood, I have always identified myself as a Muslim first, and then whatever else after that. I grew up in a nominally Muslim family, went to my local Sunday school as a kid to learn about Islam, but my upbringing wasn't particularly strict or overly religious. However, as I grew older and began to question, it wasn't long before my fascination with science really brought me to Islam. My beliefs and values, and hence my sense of identity, were always more a result of conscious effort and choice than a product of the community around me.

Since then, I have always been involved in Islamic societies and activities to a greater or lesser extent. Whilst I've always believed it is important to play an active role in my community, I've often found the views and dynamics of Muslim communities to be at odds with my own understanding of Islam. And although sometimes it is easier to conform to the majority, for me being a Muslim is not about belonging to a particular group or dressing in a certain way, but about my relationship with God, who hears and sees everything.

My journey to work on the morning of 7th July 2005 was just like any other. The first time I heard about the bombings was after arriving in the office, and we followed the news online. Official rumours that the explosions were caused by power surges were quickly dispelled by the explosion on a bus. Our office was part of an American company, so an email was promptly sent to the head office to reassure them that all staff were accounted for.

The scale of the attacks and the fatalities was not apparent to me until later on. I was 23 and more concerned about getting on with my work and the disruption to public services than anything else. I spoke briefly with my family and responded to text messages from random friends asking if I was OK, but most of this seemed like an over-reaction to me at the time. I've always been fairly sceptical about mass media and the tendency to sensationalise news, so I remained quite detached. I remember that Muslim organisations were very quick to condemn the attacks, but I wasn't sure what to make of that either.

My most vivid memory of that day was observing thousands of office workers marching off home. No tubes, no buses, just their feet to carry them. We were on the 6th floor, and we couldn't even see the pavements and roads due to the sheer number of people. And with so little traffic, it was as if they were all filing off home in complete silence. London's infrastructure may have been under attack but Londoners simply got on with it.

That day I ended up working late until 7.30pm, by which time some buses had started operating again, and so getting home was not a problem. The following morning, the tubes were running as normal, though they were definitely rather empty. I remember thinking twice before entering the tube, but that didn't stop me.

At the time, I felt impressed by London's resilience to just get up and carry on working despite the attacks. However, I'm not sure how much of this was down to resilience and how much was down to people simply not having a choice or just being so closed off to the outside world and focused on their own lives. I think all of these factors applied to me to some degree. The bombings didn't have a direct or immediate impact on me or on my day to day life. I felt victimised, but no more than 7 million other Londoners. However, subsequent events made me feel rather differently.

Two weeks later, on 21st July 2005, there were 'fake bombing' incidents at 4 tube locations, one of which happened to be my nearest tube station. There was already a heightened security environment, and for some reason it was suspected that these latest 'attacks' involved chemical or biological weapons, so a one mile security cordon was put in place. Thankfully this area didn't include my flat, but it did mean a very long walk to get home.

There have often been so-called security threats and alerts warning of attacks since 9/11, and just like Saddam Hussein's reported weapons of mass destruction, the destructive capabilities of such threats have often been grossly overstated with little or no justification. Whilst the 7th July bombings had shown that the terrorist threat to the UK was real, they did nothing to suggest that any would-be terrorists had access to chemical or biological weapons. For me, these latest security alerts were simply more over reactions and excuses for further fear mongering.

Worse was to come however. The following day, a suspected suicide bomber was pursued onto a tube train by anti-terror police and shot dead in order to prevent him from detonating a device. Initially the media reported he was male, dark-skinned or Asian-looking, wearing a large coat with wires protruding, acting suspiciously and so on. Nothing unusual then, until it was later discovered that he was actually a Brazilian. Only then were questions raised and ultimately investigations carried out into the approaches used by police.

The thing that struck me was how the public perception of the incident swiftly changed simply because of the victim's race and nationality. The picture immediately being painted of a would-be suicide bomber suddenly began to look implausible, since of course terrorists can't come from Brazil. But what if it was discovered that he was from Morocco or Yemen or Pakistan? Would the media reports have changed and the questions been raised against the police so quickly? How long would the picture-painting and police methods have been allowed to continue before any objections were heard? There would still certainly have been some investigation into any killing, but without the sudden shift in public opinion and media spotlight, I think that the immediate responses and longer term consequences could have been very different.

Of all the events during July 2005, this is probably what affected me most. Seeing an innocent man gunned down by our own security forces simply because his appearance was mistaken for that of a suspected terrorist. And seeing how perceptions of the event were turned upside-down, apparently due to the victim's racial background rather than their actual innocence or guilt.

Racial and religious profiling and media stereotyping were not new to me, and these have increased in line with 'anti-terrorism' or fear politics. However, this incident really brought home to me the fact that I was no longer safe from the police and those who were supposed to be protecting me. Not only was I a potential target for a suicide bomber from my own community, I was now also a potential target for security forces from my own government.

Violence cannot be overcome with more violence; fear cannot be overcome by more fear. The bombings were barbaric violent acts targeting innocent civilians and aiming to create fear and terror. However, if in response we effectively come down to the same level, if we also turn to violence, victimize the innocent and create fear, then surely evil has triumphed. It doesn't matter which side you are identified with, everyone loses.

As a Muslim, I could not identify with the bombers or their ideology, but events like this also bring into question whether or not I can identify with the rest of Britain either. I believe that practical steps need to be taken to prevent terrorist attacks, but does profiling and alienating the Muslim community increase or decrease the likelihood of future violence? Although these events may not have impacted on me directly, seeing the police tactics and government policies in response to the bombings made me feel as frustrated and helpless as seeing the bombings themselves.

The chain of events of July 2005 and the subsequent implications made it a difficult time to be a British Muslim, and they have led many to question their identities. However, I don't believe that events like this have to define me. I choose my identity, and it is not something that any extremist minority can hijack or that any authorities can suppress. God knows my true identity, the thoughts going through my head, the events going on around me, and the true reasons for every decision I make.

These events reminded me of the temporary and superficial nature of everything in the world around me, and that sometimes the only way to make sense of what is going on outside is to look deeper inside. These events made me feel fear, anger and frustration, but ultimately it is my faith that gives me strength to persevere and the hope for a better future.

Bin Laden's Relative?

Anjum Anwar

Anjum Anwar has a unique job as a Muslim on the staff of an Anglican cathedral. She was appointed as a Dialogue Development Officer in April 2007, to create dialogue in Blackburn, a town that has been labelled as the most segregated in the UK. Previously she served as an Education Officer at the Lancashire Council of Mosques, spearheading the 'Understanding Islam,' project in partnership with Lancashire County Council. She was awarded an MBE in 2005 for her services to the community of Lancashire. She is also Chair of Woman's Voice – a grass roots organisation for women.

"OK PEOPLE, let's get going; we have a lot of work to get through." I was speaking to approximately 60 young people, aged between 12 and 13 years old, at a Lancashire school in Garstang. It was a pleasant day, with the sun shining brightly and the young people chattering away, not listening to a word that was being spoken to them, and quite rightly too. It was one of those rare occasions when the children from Beardwood High School – a school with 99.9% pupils of Muslim background from Blackburn were meeting children from a 99.9% non-Asian school in Garstang. They had a lot to say and a lot to ask. It's not often that children of different backgrounds, in our part of the world, have an opportunity to discuss commonalities. The date was 7th July 2005 and the 'Understanding Islam' project was making links with two very different schools.

'Understanding Islam' was a project that was born out of the 9/11 atrocities. Coming from an educational background I was appointed to spearhead this venture throughout Lancashire schools, colleges and beyond. Lancashire County Council and the Lancashire Council of Mosques had decided that something had to be done to combat stereotypes of Muslims in the media given the number of racist incidents which had peaked soon after 9/11. 1.5 billion Muslims around the world were being held responsible for the atrocities committed by 19 men! I was given the task of working with more than 650 schools over a period of 12 months. Although the project would last 5 years, I knew my work was cut out. The task ahead was exciting, daunting but at the same time a challenge. 9/11 had changed many lives and had left many people with questions that were not being responded to. Unfortunately, our churches, mosques, politicians and religious leaders are brilliant at responding to questions that people are not asking! A society that forces people to call a 'black sheep' a 'rainbow sheep' has already given in to political correctness gone mad. Teachers were afraid to ask questions about Islam, or Muslims, for fear of offending and it was deemed better and easier to keep quiet rather than be challenged or to appear challenging on the subject of Islam. When I sent out letters to schools informing them that Lancashire County Council and the Lancashire Council of Mosques had appointed an education officer to come into schools to work with students and staff within the context of the Religious Education (RE) Agreed Syllabus, I received 48 requests in one day. Here was a gap that needed to be addressed, but why was there such a gap?

Working all over Lancashire bought me into contact with schools that were isolated with a very mono-culture. Information about different cultures and faiths came only from either books or television. Hence any meeting with people from different backgrounds was a novelty for their children and teachers.

Questions that were posed to me on my many visits to schools ranged from "Why are Muslim women not allowed to work?" to "Am I related to Osama Bin Laden?" I found the interaction a source of joy. However, many of the questions that were asked by young people left many staff members the colour of beetroot. One such incident was at a local Church of England school in Blackburn, when an 11 year old pupil asked me, in front of the whole school, "Are you related to Osama Bin Laden?" I took a deep breath and responded very politely "Yes." You could hear a pin drop. The young person's face dropped and the teachers were perplexed. Then I added "We are all related to each other, however, some brothers and sisters sometimes are naughty, but we need to find out why they are being naughty." Only then did the teachers' facial expressions change – with some relief, I may add.

It was precisely these questions that needed to be responded to, but it was also important how we responded. I, as a Muslim, did not need to be apologetic about my faith; rather the actions of a few criminals must not be the yardstick to measure the whole of the Muslim population. Hence, my visits to schools of all faiths and no-faith gave me an opportunity to demystify faith from culture, Islam from Muslims and more importantly these visits gave me an opportunity to respond to many questions that were important to children.

Walking into a Roman Catholic school, I was bombarded with questions about my headscarf. However, I noticed a statuette of Madonna (not the singer, thank goodness!), but that of Lady Mary, mother of Jesus (peace and blessings of Allah be upon them), looking serene and peaceful and wearing a blue head scarf. I pointed to the statuette and asked the children who she was? All hands went up to tell me that that is, "our Lady, mother of Jesus." I simply asked them "What is she wearing on her head?" The children went quiet for a few seconds and pointed to my head scarf, "She is wearing a headscarf." By bringing commonalities into the conversation, I had made a point, Mary mother of Jesus (peace and blessings of Allah be upon her) was my role model, and I was trying to live up to the high standards that she advocated, just as some of the school children probably followed David Beckham, as their role-model. Two days later I received a letter from a young pupil from this particular Roman Catholic School, with two similar drawings of two women wearing a head scarf, one said Mary and the other Anjum.

One of the methodologies that I knew would be a hit with schools was to bring children of different background together for a day and give them an opportunity to speak to each other, ask questions and learn from each other in a safe and comfortable environment.

One such day was 7th July 2005 with two schools, one from Blackburn and one from Garstang. However, this day was to change the lives of many people in the UK and beyond, and once again, the Muslim community would come under the microscope. Once again I had to look within my faith to find the courage to face difficult questions. However, on this particular day, we had the CBBC reporters with us, as they were going to film some of the activities that we had organized to bring children of different backgrounds together. At approximately 11 a.m. one of the reporters came into the class room that I was in and asked me to come outside. She informed me that there had been a bombing. My mind was racing and I did not hear her say where the bombing had taken place, except my priority was my children, all 60 of them – and as I turned to go back to the class room, she repeated that "there had been a bombing in London." I remembered gasping, because I felt that the whole point of my work at that precise moment had been hijacked. The CBBC reporter asked how I was going to deal with this. I called the rest of my team together and conferred with them, and it was decided that I should gather all the children in the canteen and speak to them, tell them the truth. However, whose truth, what was the truth?

All 60 children were gathered in the canteen, and I spoke to all of them, telling them that a terrible disaster had struck London and that at the moment we did not know how many people had been injured, but what we did know was that it was a bomb blast. There was deadly silence in the canteen then all the children started to whisper amongst themselves. Suddenly I realized that all the white children had huddled together whilst all the Muslim children were standing where they were, in smaller groups. It was almost as if they had become transfixed to the ground. At that precise moment, I remembered that on the 12th September, day after 9/11, I had walked into a shop and the shop-keeper refused to serve me, and I too had become transfixed to the floor for a few minutes, which seemed like years. I too was being punished for 9/11, somehow, I was being held responsible for all the atrocities that happened on 9/11. I had become homeless, identity less and felt I needed to run somewhere, but where? This was my home; I had nowhere else to go. I wanted to hug all the Muslim children, not because they were the only ones who felt the pain, but their pain was twinned with the fear of what the 'others' were thinking. I could almost hear them thinking "were the bombers Muslim?" I pre-empted their thoughts before they could verbalize it, and said that whoever the bombers were, they were not our friends, for anyone that can hurt innocent people cannot be our friend, and today, we are amongst friends. However, the Muslim children, at the exact moment became withdrawn and quiet and I knew that I had to get them to speak, so we decided to cancel the follow-up activities and got them onto the playing field in fresh air. As the Muslim children walked out, some of the taunts from the older children about Osama Bin Laden could be heard, but we had to deal with this head on.

Once on the playing fields we all sat around in a circle and allowed the children to ask questions and responded to them as they came in hard and fast.

The information that we needed to get through to the children was that an hour ago, they had formed some kind of 'friendship'; could we allow 'bad' people to ruin our lives, could we allow the actions of a minority of people to influence the lives of the 'majority' of people. Hitler and his people were responsible for killing six million Jews, should we hate all Germans?

Lunch time was approaching and we decided to bring the sandwiches and drinks to the playing field, so that all 60 children could be away from the rest of the school population. We felt that otherwise it would be difficult to shield the Muslim children from some unfriendly remarks, as was witnessed when the children were walking out and were taunted by some of the older children. During the lunch break we found some of the Muslim girls sitting with some of the Garstang High School girls, and as I walked towards one group of girls, I was hailed, and as I turned, a young Garstang High School girl shouted, "Hey Miss! We don't care about those people who bombed London, we are friends." She put her arm around one of the Muslim girls, and showed a peace sign. Although the Muslim girl and a boy were still feeling apprehensive, I had tears in my eyes. The action of this young girl spoke a million words. I had my camera and instantly took a photo of these young people.

The day ended with all the children gathered in the main hall to say good bye. The Muslim children were anxious to get back to their school and home. Many young girls and boys exchanged telephone numbers and email addresses, which was a sign that we had not completely lost the day. However, our hearts were heavy as we headed back to Blackburn, for we knew that we had to go through the scrutiny once again. Once again, we would need to prove that not all Muslims are terrorists, not all women wearing head-scarves were potential suicide bombers, not all young Muslim men donning beards and wearing a hat were bad men.

I did not return to my office on 7 July, as I just could not face any media attention but returned to my home, to my son. Turning on the television and listening to the information flooding in, everything was pointing towards Muslim young men who had decided to take action into their own hands. Yet no one was asking what made these young men, who had their whole future in front of them, take such drastic action. What was the catalyst that made them do what they did?

Late in the evening I switched on my laptop, as I usually would do to respond to emails. However I was not prepared for the emails abruptly cancelling my visits to the schools or putting off mosque visits, as parents were not sure "about sending their children to the mosque." I would often give mosque guided tours to school children, parents and people from statutory and non-statutory organizations. We would also sit in the mosque and have a question and answer session, highlighting the role of the mosque and what is the concept of a mosque.

I wrote back to one particular school requesting them to re-think about cancelling the mosque visit, and instead invited all the parents of the children to come with the school, or certainly those parents, who felt apprehensive about sending their children to a mosque. This paid off, and a few parents came the following week with their children to the mosque. As we were leaving the mosque, a mother turned to me and said, "thank you for the visit, I am so glad that I came, it's nothing like what I had imagined, you get so much negative information in the media."

The mosque visit was a success and my persistence had paid off. My belief in my faith gave me the strength to carry on and I know that 7/7 will forever remain a black day in our lives but it also provided me with many opportunities to set the record straight. My confirmed commitment to the following Qur'anic verse keeps me going:

"O ye who believe! stand out firmly for Allah, as witnesses to fair dealing, and let not the hatred of others to you make you swerve to wrong and depart from justice. Be just: that is next to piety: and fear Allah. For Allah is well-acquainted with all that ye do."

Quran 5:8

Reliving the Past

Murtaza Shibli

Murtaza Shibli is a trainer, writer and consultant on Muslim issues, security and conflict, and an expert on South Asia. He has worked as a journalist and security consultant. In his recent role, he worked for the Muslim Council of Britain as Public Affairs and Media Officer. As a journalist in Kashmir, he has campaigned for minority Hindu rights and spent time with scores of guerrilla resistance leaders and interviewed them along with some Afghan jihad veterans. He has an MA in Mass Communication and Journalism from the University of Kashmir and an MSc. in Violence, Conflict and Development from the School of Oriental and African Studies, London. He is also a poet and song writer, and is currently working on his first music album in his mother tongue – Koshur.

SITTING on the front seat of our second hand Volkswagen Polo estate, as my wife drove from Ealing, the road from Shepherd's Bush leading to Holland Park looked serene and calm. It was bordered by rows of tall chinars, or maple trees, which lent it a majestic look reminiscent of Srinagar's Boulevard Road, which runs along the famous Dal Lake at the foothills of Koh-e-Maran on the Indian side of Kashmir. Although I thoroughly enjoyed the setting, the full bloom of the maple spread its winged seeds all around creating unending misery for me as I am highly allergic to its pollen. The constant coughing and irritation in my eyes would continually remind me of my days at Kashmir University where I studied journalism at the Mass Communication department on Naseem Bagh Campus. This campus was surrounded by these spreading chinar trees that branched out in every direction of the vast expanse and gave it a dim and shady appearance even beneath the hot sun. We aptly named it the Siberia of Kashmir University as it was covered in frost even when winter had receded from everywhere else. Chinar, Kashmir's national tree is thought to have been brought in by the Mughals from Central Asia. The legend is that Jehangir, the Mughal emperor, planted 1200 chinar saplings at Naseem Bagh which were watered with milk regularly. These myths have romanticized these massive chinars, and have inspired much poetry. I have always struggled to appreciate its romantic beauty, as working in Holland Park brought back both the allergies and past memories of pain and violence.

My interest in violence and terror is biographic. Having grown to maturity in Kashmir in the years immediately preceding, and during the time of, the violence which intensified in 1989, killings and bomb blasts are not unique to my experience. Neither were the phenomena of extremism and radicalization; Kashmir was full of it, and many of my friends, neighbours, acquaintances or relatives were consumed by it as the politics of reason failed and bad governance led to breakdown of state structures. In the presence of unprecedented state brutality and retaliation, thousands became casualties of road side bombings, stray bullets, cross firing or custodial deaths.

When I arrived in Britain in late 2000, one of my first memories of London was a plurality of Kashmiri groups clamouring for Azadi or freedom of Kashmir in the news pages of the Urdu daily Jang, the largest circulated English/Urdu daily of the Pakistani Kashmiri community. What was surprising, the gravity of which I only understood later, was a regular occurrence of 'jihad conferences' that were held at various places at intervals, and which exhorted a new generation of British Kashmiris to fight for the liberation of Kashmir. At these conferences, several Kashmiri 'leaders' from around the world would gather, many prefixing 'maulana' to their names to signal their status as religious scholars, mostly self-appointed and of untested scholarship. They would add texture to their rhetoric by throwing in Arabic phrases, quotes from the Qur'an, interpreting God's wisdom to suit the mood music of the gathering and their own wider material and political interest. They spoke with vague enthusiasm about a future which was difficult to imagine. But the audiences felt childishly pleased with a strange sense of exhilaration in their heart, which led them deeper into beautiful and insubstantial dreams. More bizarre was the participation of many British Parliamentarians, who not only spoke against the grave human rights violations in Kashmir, but also seemed to silently approve the macabre methods of engagement with the wider world that were being proposed for their constituents by fiery leaders.

In the next few months, I came into contact with several other organizations like Hizbut Tahrir (HT) and its splinter groups. I attended my first big HT conference at London Excel sometime in late 2001; an impressive gathering of speakers and a large number of British-born Muslim men and women. Many speakers, with artfully trimmed beards, spoke about honour, revenge, blood and power. I could not recall anyone mentioning a single word of love, compassion or forgiveness; important acts of charity in the eyes of Allah. During their lectures, many of them waved their hands, accompanied by shrill voices in a well rehearsed manner, a practice I had seen scores of times before when I watched Kashmiri leaders deliver inflammatory speeches to angry young Kashmiris provoking them to run riot in the streets and fight heavily armed Indian soldiers with nothing more powerful than their youthful bodies. As I allowed myself to make comparisons in my mind, my heart was filled with dreadful foreboding, which added to my uncertainty that I have been living as a Kashmiri ever since my birth. The rhetoric filled me with terror and I grieved silently beside my wife, who had known HT since her university days on the campus. She could feel my growing unease but pretended not to notice. After the conference ended, she tried to be casual and asked me several times if I was ok? Following my usual practice from my years in Kashmir, I tried to separate my feelings from my vulnerability. Soon afterwards, following 9/11 when my Kashmiri identity was taken over by my Muslim identity as a suspect, I tried everything to insulate myself from the outside.

Some years later, walking down Southall Broadway in early June 2004, I came across a group of anti-democracy protestors from Al Muhajiroon who were running up and down the Broadway in their car which was pasted all over with posters condemning democracy with slogans such as 'Democracy go to hell'. One of the members handed me a leaflet that counselled Muslims against the ills of 'Western Democracy' and therefore exhorting them to refrain from being part of it. A brief discussion that followed led to the discovery that he too was of Kashmiri heritage. He declared elections and democracy as 'haram' or forbidden on the basis that it was not followed by the Prophet Mohammad (peace be upon him). When I tried to question him, he applied his 'Islamic wisdom' to summarily pronounce me outside of the fold of Islam. He was scornful, arrogant and hostile, but effective with his limited repertoire that would listen to nothing. It was very hard not to yield to his violent rhetoric. For a moment, I let myself go, as I began to respond to his malice by generating my own. I only stopped after a wave of guilt pierced me and I could feel my chest tightening and my heart beating against my ribcage. The weight and abrasion of his toxic discourse continues to echo, albeit sporadically, although I try hard not to dwell too much on that encounter.

During my years in the UK, I had many such encounters, but I couldn't fathom whether these were serious, or simply passing moments of dissent and difference, a fashionable anger calculated to make one popular with girls on campuses. Despite living and breathing similar experiences in Kashmir almost daily, I could not equate this rhetoric with the daily reality of London. Perhaps, it was because the ease with which everything flowed in daily life here, but I refused to acknowledge extremism or the possibility of terrorism despite vast resentments nourished by real or imagined atrocities on Muslim communities around the world, and the role Britain played in these. Or maybe I was paralysed by the risk and complexity of understanding the future living an aftermath of what I had already lived in the prime of my youth in Kashmir, something I did not want to repeat. This failure to recognize symptoms or causes of extremism within the Muslim communities of Britain continues until now, and this is also true of organizations that claim to represent Muslims. Half of the British Muslim population was born abroad, and a large number of them have shared similar experiences of violence and repression to those I witnessed in Kashmir. I sometimes wonder if this inertia is simply a defensive mechanism, a denial of the situation or its sheer gravity, for the fear of repeating it with all its deadly consequences.

The first time I seriously thought about the possibility of a terrorist attack in the UK was during my training at London Underground. It was during our health and safety training that one of our trainers briefly touched upon terrorism. He ended his speech with a curt observation: "Remember! If something can happen, it will happen." Although, it went largely unnoticed, the comment provoked a constriction of the heart I associated with catastrophe. It was not a long wait; only a few months later it became reality as it did happen.

My day started early on 7/7; I signed in for my morning shift at Holland Park tube station at around 5.45. When I first received the news, I was at the 'gateline'. Initially, we were told that there was a power failure; a standard line which we passed on to our bewildered customers who were frustrated by our own ignorance.

Amid the confusion, I frantically tried to call my father, who had come from Kashmir and used the Underground daily to travel from Ealing Broadway to King's Cross to visit the British Library. Although my wife managed to trace him, and he was unscathed, the gravity of the terror that had ripped through the Underground broke the defensive shell I had constructed in order to feel secure from my own thoughts and experiences. My dreams of realizing a secure future collapsed in the dust of those fateful explosions. I felt humiliated by my own naivety. Even worse, this time round, I failed to assuage my fears with my usual fantasies of flight.

The events of 7/7 changed everything in Britain. Reluctantly and slowly Muslims acknowledged the deep roots of extremism that pervaded every sphere of our life. Although banished from popular Islam, the extremists were very small in number; a miniscule proportion of the British Muslim population. However, they had become well organized and thrived in the back alleys of council estates and universities, because they had remained unchallenged for such a long time. 7/7 offered a chance to mainstream Islam, the vast majority of British Muslims, to pluck up courage and challenge Muslim extremists, not only by confronting their theology but also by creating a unique British Muslim or European Muslim discourse that constructs Muslim life in the reality of the European continent. It is heartening to see many old and new organizations – Muslim Association of Britain, Muslim Council of Britain, British Muslim Forum, Sufi Muslim Council and more professional organizations like City Circle and Radical Middle Way – redefining Muslim engagement both within and outside the wider society. Scores of other small and local organizations and self-help groups of Muslim men and women – professionals, students and religious scholars – have sprung up to stem the menace and form a new and nuanced understanding of Islam for new generations of Muslims who have been born and brought up in the United Kingdom.

I believe that the challenges that confront Muslims in the UK and in Europe are enormous, but with determination and 'sabr' (patience), these can be turned into positive opportunities not, only for Muslims, but for all the communities that live in the UK. The biggest challenge for Muslims in the UK is to feel confident and powerful enough to challenge the extremists who have thrived on hate, disdain for peace, tranquillity and order. The groups of extremists, no matter how small, have succeeded in advancing their worldview by exploiting the anger, hopelessness and fear generated by the flawed, unjust and opportunistic policies of our politicians. However, these failures should not be allowed to promote hatred and give rise to reactions that cast Muslims not only as outsiders, but also as a security and cultural risk to the dominant culture. These fringe groups of extremists adopt tough and provocative language only to cover their own failures to come up with constructive and credible solutions that will appeal to all Muslims. In our increasingly diverse and rich society, there are many common interests, despite the frictions and tensions that extremists from all sides seek to exploit. This needs a strong and imaginative leadership, which Muslim communities in the UK have failed so far to receive. One cannot, however, fail to appreciate that there is an increasing attempt by new Muslim groups to challenge and isolate those extremists who can be found within the Muslim community. Muslims4UK which was formed in October 2009 took a bold step and openly and forcefully challenged Islam4UK, a front group of Al Muhajiroon, regarding its proposed march that month outside Parliament. Other mainstream Muslim organisations joined with the Muslim Council of Britain (MCB) in describing the proposed march as a 'deliberate action to provoke hatred and division in society', calling upon all Muslims to ignore such provocations. The call from Muslims4UK united diverse Muslim groups from the MCB to British Muslims for Secular Democracy and forced Islam4UK to cancel the march. As Muslims are becoming more mature and gaining the confidence needed to handle their affairs with dignity and competence, fringe groups like Al Muhajiroon are becoming desperate in their rage and frustration. As I was working as the Public Affairs and Media Officer at the MCB at the time, I received a threatening email, which declared that the MCB was working for Kuffar or infidels and pronounced us all non-Muslims. Unlike the incident in Southall, I smiled wryly, since this time I did not feel isolated.

The most negative influence to challenge and demoralize Muslims is the media frenzy that followed the 7/7 atrocities, which turned a terrible tragedy into a kind of circus, playing with anything to do with Islam, twisting it in order to sell news, advance agendas and hide hatreds and phobia. The sudden and intense scrutiny of Muslims meant that one could not lead a life free from unwanted and unsolicited intrusion, even if one had nothing to do with the politics of terror or otherwise. In the immediate aftermath, I felt as if I was being watched and followed at every step of the way. I felt ridiculed by menacing news headlines that saw terror nestling in every headscarf, and every mosque as a place that peddled hatred of the rest of the society. Only a couple of days after the 7/7 atrocity I received a phone call from a journalist friend, someone who I had known for a long time. Without much introduction, he curtly asked me if I felt 'somewhat guilty' because the bombers were mostly of Kashmiri-Pakistani background. My heart sank, since I did not know how to respond. If a friend who had known me for more than a decade, and had had countless interactions with me in different settings thought I must share some blame, the whole world must think of me as sinister and as culpable as the bombers. This simplistic way of looking at things continues to be advanced by journalists and commentators, and this tempts many of our politicians to follow the lead and profit from the politics of fear. It is alarming to see our leading politicians adopt combative postures devoid of any sophistication and courtesy, and to make wild charges and claims about botched terror raids or Muslim schools. This has made growing levels of Islamophobia and anti-Muslim violence not only acceptable but also fashionable, and many intellectuals have also raised their voices, ostensibly under the guise of the freedom of expression.

A couple of months after the tragedy, a time when any middle eastern looking man was considered a security threat, my first experience of being a 'potential terrorist' occurred. I was at Westminster Tube station, when two police officers stopped me. They took me to the side of the Westbound District Line platform, and carried out a full body search. They detained me for nearly an hour, asking questions, scrutinizing every bit of paper in my rucksack and even flipping through every page of the book I was reading at that time – strangely, 'Salonica: City of Ghosts' by Mark Mazower, desribing how, under the Ottomans, the town of Salonica thrived amid racial harmony between Muslims, Christians and Jews. I had highlighted several passages and made my own comments, much to the suspicion of prying coppers. Hundreds of passengers watched me being questioned as I reminded myself of scores of similar but worse experiences in Kashmir. This calmed me down a bit, but ruined my planned dinner with my wife, who was waiting for me at Ealing, worrying endlessly. By the time we met at Ealing Broadway tube station, our appetites had all but vanished. When I came home tired and drained, I looked at myself in the bathroom mirror and cursed my 'terrorist' looks. To make it worse, I hadn't shaved for a few days and the stubble had definitely shaped me to fit the 'terrorist mould'. For a moment I even started doubting myself. The only consolation that I drew from this experience was that I was given a 'receipt' – a yellow paper as a proof of my roadside search and release, duly signed by the one of the officers. This was a million times better than in Kashmir, where many such roadside checks would end up with people's disappearance and their subsequent mutilated dead bodies resurfacing on the roadside or recovered from the Jhelum River, often unrecognizable. The content of my 'yellow receipt' was not that encouraging, though. The police officer who handed me the 'receipt' had stated the reason for my 'stop and search' as 'related to terrorism'. Incidentally, according to the copy of search record I was given, I was wearing a black coat and black trousers with brown shoes and short black hair. The 'grounds for authority' were described as 'carrying a black rucksack' with the officer in-charge writing in the column 'Object(s) of search' as 'articles for use in Terrorism Act'. Thankfully, as stated in the search record, my clothes were not removed nor were my intimate parts exposed.

In the aftermath of 7/7, my personal experiences have varied. While one of my friends wanted to know if I felt guilty, many others were sympathetic and supportive, and listened patiently to my frustrations as the painful experience of fellow Muslims. There was a greater understanding among my university professors or friends who had seen all this, when it happened to the Irish, at the height of IRA activities. However, this has not prevented me from noticing anti-Muslim feelings and rhetoric, which emanates regularly, even from members of my extended family, a good number of whom are not Muslim. Only a couple of months after 7/7, sitting down at a relative's house in a Paris suburb, one of their paying guests, an Indian electrician, knowing that I was a Kashmiri, started talking about 'Islamic terrorism' in Kashmir. Not knowing that I was a Muslim, he went on to say that all the Muslims are evil and terrorists and deserve to be consigned to gas chambers as Hitler had done to the Jews. He was quick to sympathize with Jews, but appreciated the method adopted by Hitler could prove useful and worthy of emulation. Occasional offensive remarks and subtle disparaging observations, humorous put downs, sarcastic tones of voice, disapproving looks and innuendoes have become part of life. In one of our visits to a craft show in Surrey, my wife and I met a wonderful old couple. They hospitably sat us down for a cup of tea. However, as soon as they came to know about our Muslim identity, the lady was quick to say, with a forced grin, that they were not infidels. Just a few weeks ago, I came to know that one of my non-Muslim relatives addressing my year old son, Sulaiman, had said: 'I know you are a Paki (Muslim), but I still love you to bits'. Then he kissed my son who acknowledged his appreciation with a gorgeous wide smile.

Being a Taliban

Anisa Abouelhassan

Anisa Abouelhassan is the CEO of Muslim Comms, an independent engagement, project management and communications consultancy. She is a volunteer on the London board of the Crimestoppers Trust, formerly working as the Asian-Muslim Communities Manager for the organization. Anisa is a qualified development worker whose interests are in tackling the injustices of all kinds of criminality that harm communities. She is an English revert to Islam and lives in Surrey with two young children.

First of all I would like to seek forgiveness from God for any mistakes I make in my writing; some of the lessons I have learned since 7/7 are that the words and actions of one Muslim can reflect positively or negatively on all British Muslims. All views here are my own, and I don't claim to represent any organisation or any other Muslim.

On 7/7, I was at work in the youth offending services office in the North East of England, when the news of the incidents in London, started to spread around the office. It was not until lunch time when I was able to look at the news online that I found that it was bomb attacks.

Travelling home, I wondered about the victims, were there any mums killed? I'm a mother and I couldn't dare to imagine the pain, such a death would cause to a family. How were people getting home, was anyone I know hurt or worse? I imagined the streets of London like scenes out of the movies with streets that were deserted and filled with an eerie silence.

I remember thinking to myself, "Please God don't let this have any Muslim involvement". I also remember thinking "I'm glad I no longer wear the veil". Post 9/11 and pre 7/7, whilst veiled I had encountered a number of Islamophobic incidents.

Having a train carriage full of drunken football fans, serenade me with a chorus of "Taliban, Taliban, Taliban" was one of the lighter experiences.

Some days before 7/7 I had received an e-mail of a video link of an Iraqi women being raped by occupation soldiers. I'm a regular reader of online forums and blogs; so I knew then that people were so angry and frustrated about world events. I have lived amongst Arabs, I have Arab family members and I have spent enough time staying in Muslim majority communities to know the upset that world events had caused and I knew how invading Iraq had hurt the pride of the Arabs and the hearts of many people, not only Muslims.

Even so, it was then still beyond my own contemplation that British Muslims could play any part in causing events such as 7/7. On finding out it was British Muslims, I thought it must have been some kind of conspiracy. It took a lot of inward contemplation and research to admit to myself that it was British Muslims who had carried out 7/7. Worse still it was British Muslims and a revert to Islam who had caused so much pain.

I'm a British white revert to Islam. For me Islam has no contradiction with social justice, harmony and respect for all human life. I reverted in my early teens after having contact with Muslims and then went on to university to study development and in doing so worked in a range of community organisations trying to better the life chances of other human beings. I'm an idealist, this is something ingrained in my character, and I value humans having a quality of life that means they can fulfil their aspirations. To find that there were British Muslims who would take the lives of others in such a way, saddened me in ways words cannot express.

I started working in Muslim voluntary organisations at the age of eighteen, and have preferred to be a quiet gardener. I have always known there were many social problems in British Muslim communities such as poverty, crime, lack of capacity in organisations, and the treatment of women. I have preferred to get on with helping to sort them out rather than stand up and shout about them or schmooze up to any particular government policy or group of the day in order to score political points. 7/7 heightened the need to get on with trying to sort out these social problems quicker. It also was a reminder that the capacity of Muslim organisations to try and carry out enormous tasks alone and voluntarily is not enough.

In my development work I have also found there is so much in-fighting amongst Muslim groups and that the best way to get things done was not to belong to a particular group but to work with all who hold wider social common values such as community cohesion, peacefulness and transparency. I believe in dialogue and have had one to one conversations with Muslim leaders and told them at times some uncomfortable home truths. Being frank, particularly about the effectiveness of organisations or, for example, their lack of females within the management structure, however uncomfortable at times for individuals, has not hindered my opportunities to work for change. Since 7/7 there have been a number of British Muslim organisations who have tried to develop their capacity and be less insular in doing more good works and I hope as a development worker that this continues to be the case.

I was previously the Asian-Muslim Communities Manager for the Crimestoppers Trust, helping to fight all kinds of crime, including terrorism within British Asian-Muslim communities. Muslim communities are disproportionately affected by crime both as victims and perpetrators. I see all crime as an injustice and although I am no longer a staff member at Crimestoppers, I know the great results it has as a charity in fighting crime so I continue to volunteer as a member of the London board.

In order to stop any potential 7/7 happening again, I believe that law enforcement, voluntary organisations and the Muslim community have much more long term work to carry out together. 7/7 has made me realise that there is need for more Muslim police officers or those individuals who are very good at working within Muslim communities to work in counter terrorism. I have seen and experienced the effects of Islamophobia, counter terrorism policies, strategies and incidents on Muslim communities and I know at times relationships between individual Muslims, communities and law enforcement have been strained. As I have worked and continue to work closely with law enforcement, I know law enforcement officers as individuals and I know how individuals can genuinely care about their communities and stopping crime, regardless of race, religion or any other factor. This is why one of my passions is also to help law enforcement across the UK to work with Muslim communities effectively with honesty and integrity in tackling crime issues. There needs to be better communications so that when individual incidents do occur that they are dealt with as individual incidents that do not reflect on the law enforcement service or the whole Muslim community.

75

In the months following 7/7, I thought a lot about how it could have occurred: what was in the mindset of the bombers? I remember the extremist leaflets which were around in my university days and the fact that as a new Muslim I was fair game to all those groups and individuals who wanted to influence me with their sects or their versions of Islamic practice and thought. I figured that would account for the presence of a Muslim revert in the group of bombers. No matter what I had read or the conversations I had heard, or the talks I had attended, no one could influence me to hurt another human being. The conclusion which I came to was that the bombers were psychopathic murders who had sought to justify their urges to kill by violently politicising Islam. I also concluded that there is a problem with a very small minority of Muslim individuals who would advocate violent extremism, and it will take the help of people from all backgrounds to constructively help to tackle the problem.

I have researched a lot about the victims of 7/7. There are the individuals' stories which have profoundly affected me, particularly the one about the mother of a victim, who left the church as she couldn't forgive the 7/7 bombers after her daughter was killed. I don't know if I could forgive anyone if they hurt my children, all I can do is pray God forbid. The ways in which the families of those who died or those who were injured have suffered are painful stories to hear or read. I read their blogs and watch with interest when they speak on TV or listen intently to them on the radio. I feel it would be beneficial in stopping violent extremism to hear more from those who were so affected, as it deeply affects me to think of how compassionate, strong and humanistic many of the victims of 7/7 are, including those who say that they don't blame our faith and they work now so that lessons will be learned for everyone. They have powerful voices. These stories of victims of crime no matter what their background remind me to work hard for social change. Sometimes when I know that I haven't spent enough time with my family and I'm having guilty mother syndrome, I remember some of the victims of crime such as 7/7 and it keeps me motivated to keep helping in any way I can to affect change.

After 7/7, an Islamophobic witch hunt started to happen in some parts of the media. There were so many so called 'terror' or 'Islam' experts around, neo conservative, fascist and anti Islamic; think tanks, ex-jihadi spokespeople, lobby and campaign groups flourished overnight. Newspaper columnists, bloggers and radio hosts wanted to write about topics such as Islamic polygamy, forced conversions, stoning, female genital mutilation, forced marriage, constantly associating Islam and terrorism. Overnight, many of the people who spoke for and about Islam in the media were individuals linked with negative 'Islamic cultural' experiences. As a development worker I welcomed the dialogue, but there was not enough balance in the coverage and many voices were marginalised. Individuals and Muslim organisations who were already struggling with capacity building were being attacked left right and centre. In the British media, controversial figures who advocated violent jihad and social division were given so much airtime; ideally they should have been ignored until the point that they broke the law and then put into jail, as they would have been in other countries. I felt many were providing platforms for extremists who would continue to make the lives of British Muslims even more difficult after 7/7.

I was asked, and continue to be asked, to discuss controversial topics or things that are seen as 'Islamic or Muslim social ills' with friends, family, neighbours, and colleagues. To me, these social ills are not the Islam that is a part of me and others. Islam is a source of goodness and all this stereotyping and box fitting can make individuals feel alien to Britain. The 'social ills', whatever they may be, just happen to be affecting some Muslims. Nevertheless, they need to be dealt with and there are many people trying.

It's natural that 9/11 and 7/7 would cause a surge in interest about Islam and Muslims. As a Muslim it has made me grow to the point where I'm confident enough to discuss aspects of my faith with others. I understand why people would want to discuss Islam and they may have varied reference points of understanding. I'm confident enough to express my views to someone, particularly when they are being offensive in their ignorance or intolerance, in a way that will not lead to a fire fight of words or cause a break down in dialogue.

I remember watching a programme about a British white Muslim revert woman who had decided to leave the UK after 9/11 happened as she felt that the Western world would turn against Muslims. I understood that feeling after 7/7 and did at one time contemplate leaving the UK not for myself but for my children. The reason that I decided not to leave the UK is that this is my country, full of people, history, systems and ways which I love and cherish. I'm proud to be British and see no contradiction between being Muslim and British.

Life in the UK is more of a struggle now for Muslims; it's even harder to be positive about the future of British Muslims in society. British Muslims will for some time be a 'suspect' community for many people. I can understand how this treatment can make some people upset, particularly those who have suffered injustices in the so called 'war on terror'. I too have been a 'suspect'; a suburban Surrey woman who had to spend extra time in airport security, whilst officers prod through my children's food asking me to drink their bottled milk, with two grumpy young children in hand.

After 7/7, I could and still do understand why people would fear and hate Islam because of 7/7 and why there are groups of individuals who would only want to see, hear and spread negativity about Islam and British Muslims. I've matured to the point where I no longer shout at the TV in frustration. The British Muslim community with the help and support of humanistic individuals have also gained more political awareness and have sought new ways to be a part of debates rather than being unrepresented, particularly when being debated. The number of Muslim columnists in the media has now grown but there is still a need to hear Muslims discuss more issues that affect all citizens, not just Muslims.

Also there are growing numbers of people who are defending British Muslims against fascists, whether that is by what they write, what they say or by how they march. I personally view those who defend the rights of Muslims to live peacefully as equal British citizens, as heroes; sometimes we would never know their names but it's their goodness in what they do to bring peace and understanding to British society. It's the deeds and actions of these heroes from all backgrounds which are rebutting the capacity of violent extremists or those who use faith and ethnicity, though inaccurately, to divide society. They are the most effective tools for social cohesion.

FROM COVERT TO CONVERT
'WHO, WHAT & WHY
I WAS LED TO BELIEVE.'

MUHAMMAD AMIN

Muhammad Amin was born in 1976 in Dublin, Ireland. Showing a predilection for drawing and writing as a young boy, he went on to be educated in Visual Communications in the midlands of his home country. He then spent ten years in Edinburgh, where he developed his interest in Arts – performance poetry, theatre and graphic art – being employed mostly in a community work context. He spent some time with a Christian community group there, before seeking to confirm his belief in Islam. He now resides in Norwich, Norfolk, with his wife, and they are expecting their first child. He continues to explore his interests in creative writing and graphic arts.

THE consequences of power must be seen to be understood. Its darker machinations must be understood to be seen. Those who have faith in the unseen are not the blind, for that is those who believe all they see.

An 'anarchist camp' (no, an eco-village – I was there) at midnight. We had come to Gleneagles in the back of a van having done a play in Glasgow's Barrowlands, and previous to that in Edinburgh's Festival Theatre. The play was about the 2001 G8 Summit in Genoa, where the carabinieri dealt blows to peaceful protestors, in the course of pursuing the more active members. Some had reportedly shot a young man, driven and then reversed over his body, before driving off. That night, they made an incursion into Indymedia's offices, and beat everyone they found. I had heard of this, but doing the play and seeing the footage included in it brought it to me more vividly. I also put these events in the context of a world in which one month later, the Twin Towers would be destroyed. In politics, I only saw the anger then, never the intrigue.

As we arrive at the village, quasi-militant minds meet at a marquee – more green than beret. They are dressed in black; they have no lights – the 'black block' who stain the camp with their name. Anyone who turns up to a protest in black, and looks like they are in a civil war, forms part of a battalion. Somehow, from this gathering of strangers, a leader emerges. A man with an American accent seems to be tonight's spokesman by silent consensus. The plan is simple. There on a flipchart in the dim light is a cursory agenda. The place is surrounded by police. The more cavalier are urged to ride out, before more police arrive. I and my friends have only just ridden in, so we watch as an hour later, this panoply is mustered on a dirt-track – one group armoured by wheelie-bin lids, in tortoise-shell formation, an offshoot of Centurion field-tactics. They sport a banner with a rallying phrase in Spanish, and tramp out the gate. We went to bed. In the morning, we hear they had walked straight up the road and into a detachment of police. It had rained during the night, so the action was a washout. The supposed enclosure by police was a figment of imagination. We walked out the gates and got on a bus to Gleneagles. To this day I wonder if that 'spokesperson' was an infiltrator.

Police stopping people – even pre-arranged demonstrations – from travelling. Why? Just because. Aamer Anwar threatens a legal response. But he's been defending controversial people – he's getting a reputation. Those at the heart of a struggle, from a distance, are seen to be mad. This will take months to resolve. Justice is dealt with very judiciously.

A Chinook helicopter landing on a hillock, opening its rear bay, to let bobbies from all over the country, in Day-Glo jackets, spill out. A myriad of restless characters sloganeering, at a stand-off with law enforcement. A few rush across the fields to the barricades, and start to pull them down, or climb them. It's futile, it is pawns versus knights and rooks, but there's always one. Who does he play for? Riot police, dressed in black, carrying batons and shields slowly sweeping across a field in a line. They come across some large puppets – caricatures of the various pseudo-leaders in discourse somewhere out beyond the neighbouring fields – and together make a scene which blurs the real and unreal. I had helped load these puppets onto a van the night before. This was grand theatre, and the crowd were murmuring. The murmur became a boo, and I left before the final curtain fell.

Arriving back in Edinburgh at about 1:00 in the morning, I had left my keys in a bag in the house of a friend who was by now in bed, and I was standing at my front door when I realised. I considered visiting the campsite for other returning protestors down the road, and took a walk. Imagine, me the one who had a flat in the neighbourhood, hoping to talk my way into a visitor's tent. But at the campsite, the lights were off. Stupid idea. Perhaps I was still in a newly-awakened state after the Gleneagles Summit. A state in which assumptions were distractions. I lived in what used to be one of the poorest areas in Europe, and still had repercussions of Edinburgh's heroin-induced days. This ghetto had in some ways remade me, in the six years I spent in and out of its derelict dens, and I settled for a cold concrete floor at the bottom of a neglected, scarred stairway. The world order around me was crumbling, but I clung to faith. I had been on many protests and demonstrations – I had trucked a bit with Socialist Workers Party (SWP), but was now applying my artistic sensibilities to a Christian Community, though I had yet to confirm my belief. I had read of the Disciples insurrection against Imperial occupation – by words or by deeds, and the irony that a man with a beard who rode about the Middle East on the back of a donkey would challenge the hegemony of an empire was not lost on me. That 'Render unto Caesar what is Caesar's' did not mean relinquishing worldly power to the state, but did mean that if you opt into a monetary currency, you will pay accordingly. That fundamentalists deploying a twelve-foot high Abrams tank flying the Star of David would project the idea that a boy with a sling and stone was now a modern-day Goliath showed me that truth was in the opposites. That for the richest country in the world to be bombing the poorest country in the world had me fixated on the phrase 'Blessed are the poor'. My sensibility now was moving from broad religious ideas and themes – the hieroglyphs and Egypt, the Book of Revelation and modern-day Apocalyptics which I expressed by way of costume design in Notting Hill carnival – to a real crisis of faith. What did I believe in? So I came away from the gyrating writhing hips of Afro-Caribbean women – the 'wining' dance which was outlawed by the French Colonials whose masque balls and upper-class sentimentality had spurred Carnival into being – and dwelt more on the Bible and its message. Then, as the War of Terror unfolded, I had come to disquiet yet again. I was seeing it all now in its religious significance – a false pope on a false pulpit, calling all nations to war: 'Come and see'. There were fundamental things missing from my life, which were not prescribed in the Bible, and so its lessons became, for me, a passage through artistic interpretation. The prophetic taught me there could be meaning and a political dimension to what a man of little faith might call 'life as art'. Now, having internalised that assertion, and transcending it, moving beyond the concept, I wanted a real way to say 'I believe'. That was 'where I was at', lying on a cold, concrete floor, the morning after 7/7, contemplating what I had seen, and what it all meant.

I was only ever told of the attacks in London. I was never a victim, a protagonist, a sympathiser, or a witness to them. I was only ever told. And I was told by a person who told me to watch it on an electronic device which sits in the corner of many people's domiciles — but not mine. The same device that had reported the destruction of the Twin Towers four years previous, the Guildford pub bombings as having been accredited to the IRA, the Belgrano incident, and Thatcher's assertion that it was not in hostile waters, the Gulf of Tonkin, the Man on the Moon, the scandal, the sleaze, the cartoons, the glitz, the glamour, the hype and hyperbolic sound bites. I wouldn't listen to that. I wanted food for thought — I avoided microwave dinners.

I did read of it, though. Since the War of Terror had begun, and especially with the invasion of Iraq, I had begun to read the Guardian and listen more to Radio 4 — in between spray-painting walls, doing performance poetry and working in primary schools. I started to take on more the burdens of the world. I saw the stories simply as stories, for story is where history comes from, and here I was seeing history made. So what, then, was history? It was not at an end. Those people who had read Huntington as if this was a new stage in a new millennium had not heard the clamour during World War II of 'the end of history' — that idiom was a rewrite. Like the endless trumpeting of the End of Days.

I read that the 'torpedo attack' on the US warship in the Gulf of Tonkin, the incident which allowed America to go to war with Vietnam, did not happen. That the Belgrano was in hostile waters. That the Guildford Four were released because the police had withheld evidence from the defence, and that people who said they had in fact committed the crime were dismissed. I read that the Man on the Moon was done on stage for the papers. That Secret Societies are running the country (but what is a Secret Society in a society of secrecy?). I read that Sunnis never liked Shia, that the Taliban are mad, that the neo-cons are fascist, that Jesus never lived, but he had a son. I read it all, and I don't know what to believe. I know it's not true. It's not true because I wasn't there. It's history. Streams of consciousness to take us to a universal, great expanse, on which we float, or in which we drown. I had to set sail, and give my ship a name. I did not build the ship, it was there, opportune. The waters around it were chopping at its wood, and I would simply have to put faith in its maker, if I wished to leave this parched desert of brick and glass and stagnant monumentalism. On this side, the grass was not even green any more.

The chambers of my heart had already divided what was true from what was false – or more, political ends from ideological intention. I believed in God. I believed in Jesus and the Prophets. To say Islam was causing this aggression was simply a non-Muslim's point of view, and was not based on humane experience; it was echoing the printed word. If I was to enter Islam, I would not be obliged to join the mujahedeen. I liked poetry, calligraphy and, if needs be, my visual art could take on a non-idolatrous form (that is 'idol' = 'image' = 'likeness'), and would be abstract or geometric or purely literary. There, that was settled, and the London bombings would not derail my conviction, though I can see that I will have to come to terms with these events if I am to justify myself to others.

'Religion causes all wars'? Two World Wars, the Cold War, Vietnam, Gulf Wars, Crimea, Algeria, etc., etc.? Do we blame World War II on the Jews, then? Is Russia not atheist? Saddam was a pan-Arabist and Socialist before he said the Shahada. Is a Pentagon General a model Christian simply because he attends a Seventh Day Adventist church and talks religious rhetoric? That is the 20th Century. The Crusades? There was only one group of knights who were properly representing the Vatican in Jerusalem – the Templars – and they were diplomats across the board of Abrahamic faiths. The 'Wars of Religion'? There were Catholics and Protestants on either side. Northern Ireland? You believe kneecapping, punishment beatings, executions and segregation were all a response to issues of the Sanctity of Saints and what language Mass was spoken in?

Yet 'Religion is the opiate of the masses'? Well, something contradicts there – what opiate induces a desire for war? I can't imagine a man slumping on a couch in a chemical-induced bliss being fit for the field. 'The source of all evil'? Where then is your understanding of the word coming from? 'God does not exist'? There is no debate – for those who believe, he does, for those who don't, he does not. So do you believe or not? If not, to what end is faith? Physicists point to a singularity complex, and are only recently talking of, dark matter, dark energy, and so on. It seems they are still in the dark. How does scientific theory compare with faith?

So no ideological outlook or terrorist incident deterred me from my intention. I had determined that I was a Muslim; I merely needed the opening to affirm it. I went to the mosque, but it did not seem inviting. A month after the London bombings, I went to the market – a 'mela' in Edinburgh – and met a

Scottish-born man of Pakistani parentage (let's call him 'a Muslim'). He had some calligraphy for sale, so I browsed, but was actually checking his attitude out. I got talking to him, and soon told him where I was going – I just did not know how to get there. I was heading on a trip to Turkey, so we would meet when I got back.

A US aircraft carrier docked on the south coast of Turkey. It looms half – maybe a whole – kilometre away, threatening to block out the Mediterranean sun. A clanging and thumping resounds from the bulk-headed behemoth, as men go to work. War is over the horizon. This coast is often frequented by the elite of Turkey. On a summer night it looks like a British tourist resort. The same music plays to the same popular drone. Young Turks approach alluring foreigners, will seduce and induce to worldly gains. Some soldiers are out on the town, and I go out with some Turkish people working at the hotel. On the following afternoon, I go scuba-diving, and some of the Marines are on the boat. I have read so much about this war, but I do not want them to hear my understanding, I only want to know. I must sit beside them. Whether they cannot say or will not say, I do not know, but they do not say where or when they are moving. My questions can only go so far, and in a contemplative pause, a Marine wants to show me a picture of the breasts of an army woman which he has on his phone. I look at the phone – the sun skips across the screen and light dances a blinder in my eyes. 'Nice' I say, as if I have seen. Something else is playing on my mind. I only know I am a world away from knowing.

I say my Shahada in the New Year, and within one year my whole grasp of world events would take some fundamental turnarounds. I meet a relative of the man who was convicted of the 1993 World Trade Centre attacks, and I see that the analysis of that event goes against the idea that he was guilty. I see now that belief in the official stories behind these terrorist incidents is essentially a leap of faith – they are, in fact, conspiracy theories. No evidence has ever been presented which satisfies the American Government's assertions about the 1993 incident. The same for 9/11 – no funding trail, no identification (apart from Mohammed Atta's passport found at the bottom of the Tower – do you believe in miracles?) – in fact several of those claimed to be on those planes have been found alive and well! Bin Laden denied involvement in the attacks (according to CNN News). The Pentagon only showed a blurred video of him congratulating the attackers, and it looks more like Oscar the Grouch than Osama bin Laden. No physical evidence has ever been recovered. Implicating evidence of the official story behind 7/7 has been lost or not presented. It is now academic fact that, during the Cold War, NATO conducted terrorist attacks against Italian civilians as a bulwark against creeping Communism. This 'stay-behind army' strategy was – and may still be – operational all over Europe. Communism has now collapsed, and NATO is struggling against a group of people on horseback with an SUV and the scantiest of arms. In Iraq, a couple of British soldiers are found with Arab garbs and explosives in a carved-out car, and taken into a prison for questioning. The British army performs a ram-raid with a tank on the prison wall, releasing up to 100 other prisoners, before taking the soldiers from the state body they are there to support, and being petrol-bombed by angry witnesses. In Turkey, 83 stand trial for alleged involvement in a 'deep state' plot called Ergenekon, seeking to undermine the Islamic Party there. They are found with a cache of explosives, and the Guardian reports that they were intending to dress up as Muslims when they committed the acts. I have just returned from the country of my birth – Ireland – with a book on the 'Jubilee Plot', which was an attempt by the British Government to assassinate Queen Victoria and blame it on the Irish, to undermine the move for Home Rule. When the English pay homage to the miraculous discovery of The Gunpowder Plot, I assert that he was set up, so that the incoming ruler had license to persecute a religious group at home and further his own ends, both within the nation, and at war abroad. It is not the End of History, for the story is still being spun.

FIGHTING
STEREOTYPES

SAIYYIDAH ZAIDI

Saiyyidah Zaidi is the eldest of four girls who were born and raised by her mother in North London. She is a qualified architect and a Fellow of the Association of Project Management, currently working in local government as an Assistant Director. She is also Chair of Governors of a comprehensive secondary school in East London, as well as a governor of an independent primary school. Saiyyidah is married with two children and lives in London.

IT was an ordinary, sunny day. I was in a meeting at a school with the bidder where we were discussing the designs for a new school building; we were looking at options for furniture for the classrooms. I drove to work, my husband took the tube. The meeting started at 9am and was due to end at 11. We were having a serious but jovial meeting, as we always did! At 9.45 the meeting was interrupted – someone came into the meeting looking really unwell and said some words that I can't really remember now. Bombs had gone off on the tube and bus network. We were all in shock and started to shake. The school staff asked us to go into the staff room while they were busy trying to contact parents to let them know their kids were OK and also check if parents were fine. A TV had been bought into the staff room so that staff could see what was happening. We just sat and watched in horror. I was in an all boys secondary school in south east London, probably the only hijab-wearing woman in the school; it was so obvious that I was a Muslim. I felt as if people were looking at me for my view on things – "Why did they do it, did it really say it was OK to do this kind of thing in Islam?" I am not an Aalimah (female scholar) – I am just a regular human being who is seeking the same things in life as everyone else. What were people expecting me to say? That I agreed with it? I sat there in as much shock and horror as everyone around me, shocked that this could happen in London and on buses and tubes that were so familiar.

I tried to get hold of my husband. I can't remember if I got through to him straightaway or if it took a while, but the point was that he was alright. He worked in central London and would have probably travelled part of the journey somewhere near the incidents. The next call was to my sister who worked in Old Street; it also took a while to get through to her. I think they shut down the mobile network for a few hours and we were worried as she worked in Old Street. Eventually we got through and she was OK.

My daughter was born in 2004 and I was in the early stages of my second pregnancy. I struggled to think of what kind of world we were living in. I knew we had problems in London and in the UK, but this? I think at some point most people must have thought back to 9/11 and where they were at that time – my life then was so different. I didn't wear a hijab – I was still proud to be Muslim but my 'Muslimness' wasn't externally displayed so there was no expectation for me to express a view to others or have to 'answer' for my faith. This time it was very different and I didn't like why I was being asked to give a view but also why I felt like I had to justify my decision to believe in Islam.

And here I was in the early stages of my second pregnancy wondering and worried about what the world would look like in six months time when my son would be born. How would the children of a British Asian woman and a white British man be treated?

My colleagues and I were in a leafy part of South London and, had it not been for the media, we wouldn't have had much connection with what was happening a few miles away. Travelling was going to prove an ordeal as there were no buses and no tubes, but at least we were alive and fine. I drove into work and so at least I could start to make the journey back. My work colleagues weren't sure how they were going to get home so we decided, after things were a bit clearer, that I would drive them to central London and then go and pick up my sister and take her home.

I just wanted to go home and see my loved ones; sometimes, even if you hear their voices and know that they are OK, you won't believe it until you see them in the flesh. My daughter had just had her first birthday and I was desperate to see her and hold her. I had only been back at work for a few months and it was difficult to be away from my daughter. However, I had the comfort of knowing that she was safe at nursery, even though I couldn't phone the nursery due to the phone network being shut down. If I was honest I would say that at no point had I questioned my decision to go back to work to a job that I loved, but I have always said that I need to make sure my family are safe and happy. I was not sure that this was the case on that particular day and I started to question my decision to go back to work.

We drove into central London. I was with a furniture provider and an educationalist from the local authority. We were listening to the radio in stunned silence. We shared a journey that was quite profound and moving. My passengers were white British and I still wonder how they felt about the journey – did they accept my offer of the lift because it was the only choice, or would they rather have not travelled with a Muslim in a hijab on a day when it was the Muslims that were being blamed for creating all this chaos as they detonated bombs in the heart of London? I hope that they took the lift in the spirit that it was offered – from one human being to another in a situation where we were all distressed. Did it make me feel better because I offered the lift? No, it was just the right thing to do. What did make me angry was the abuse I received after I dropped my passengers off when sitting in traffic trying to get home to my family and loved ones, a bit like most other Londoners that day.

REFLECTIONS

I remembered the IRA used to bomb London when I was younger and the events of 7/7 reminded me of when I woke up in the middle of the night as I had heard the IRA bomb that went off on the North Circular. The fear of both was similar; it was the fear of the unknown. But what was different then was that I was younger, naive and perhaps didn't really understand the political ramifications of what was being done. Now I was older and to others appeared to be guilty by association as I too was a Muslim. I can't remember thinking that all Irish people were responsible for the IRA bombing. I applied to Queen's University in Belfast to study and a teacher at my school advised that I would be asked what religion I was. I replied "Muslim." He said "No, you will either be a Catholic Muslim or a Protestant Muslim!" Now, I was just a Muslim!

My husband chose to become Muslim about one year before we met. A white British man, he was stopped during the period of IRA bombings as he looked

Irish; now he is stopped as he fits the profile of a Muslim – because of his clothing and his beard. I bet if he shaved off his beard and wore a suit and tie he would no longer be stopped, but perhaps I am just being superficial.

In the following weeks and months, I was pleased that I travelled to work by car; at least I didn't have to face the fear of the tube. I worried about strangers accusing me of carrying a bomb because I had my gym kit in a rucksack. No more rucksacks for Muslims travelling on the tube or in London. My sister was spat at and given dirty looks on the tube in the following few weeks, all because she was overtly Muslim and wearing a rucksack (with her lunch, a couple of books and work files!). She had to change her bags because of the stereotypes and fears of others.

At the time and in the following months I felt as if I constantly had to defend my free choice of religion. I am a Londoner born and bred, I pay my taxes, want my kids to do better than I did, eat fish and chips, but I also pray 5 times a day, wear a headscarf and believe in God – no contradictions for me to be a Londoner and a Muslim so why are there for others? Why do I have to defend my choice of religion and explain to people that I am not 'like them'? I strongly believe that I can be both British and Muslim and that there is no contradiction – I have a right to say 'I was born in this country and I am proud to be British', but to this I would add 'and I am proud to be Muslim'. Some people (especially external colleagues) judge the hijab (not me) when they see me at work until I demonstrate my ability to do the job. I have to justify my reason for being in the room, rather than being allowed to be because I have been employed to do a job. This has changed in the last few years, but is more apparent since I started to wear a headscarf.

NOW AND THE FUTURE

For me, Islam is a religion that promotes rights for women – I can work if I choose to, I can even keep all my earnings! I suspect that many people reading this didn't know this but there are many things that people don't know about Islam. I hope to raise my children to understand what Islam truly requires of its believers which includes contributing to the society in which we live and being active citizens.

During the day it became clear that innocent Muslims also died in the bombings – all communities in London were affected – the bombs hadn't just targeted non-Muslims, although it seemed like this was partly forgotten in some of the backlash.

A long time ago I decided that God had given me a chance and that I have had a wonderful education and excellent experiences, so I have a social responsibility to give something back to the community. I am a governor of an inclusive comprehensive school in east London and, until recently, was an independent director of a housing management organisation. I do this for two reasons – one so that I can genuinely give back to the community, but also so that hijab-wearing Muslim women are not all seen to fit the horrible stereotype portrayed by the media and press. I want to contribute to the country in which I was born, raised and choose to live. In this country I am not seen to be British because of my colour; when I last visited Pakistan in 1996, I was not seen as Pakistani because I was born in the UK: so what do I do? One of the battles I face is that actually I am a citizen of the world, not just Britain. The events of 7/7 reminded many British citizens that we are also citizens of the world and are affected by wider issues. My view for the future is that I just carry on trying to be the best citizen of London, Britain, Europe and the world whilst being the best Muslim that I can be. And with my husband I will raise my children to do the same.

A Day of Sorrow

Imam Mohamed Rawat

Imam Mohamed Rawat is a second generation Gujarati Muslim born in Nuneaton, Warwickshire, in the late 60s. He moved to Hackney, London, at the age of 12, where he attended secondary education. In 1984 he went to study at an Islamic institute in Lancashire where he completed his studies in various Islamic subjects including theology and jurisprudence. Since his graduation he has been an active religious leader for the community in North Hackney in various capacities. These include working voluntarily in roles such as a public school governor, mentoring young boys in football, as well as promoting peace and community cohesion with the Metropolitan Police and other local religious leaders of different faiths.

M Y memories of 7/7 are very vague. I know that the news of the event did not immediately reach me although I cannot recall why. When I did eventually hear about it in the afternoon, I was walking on the local high street when a Muslim who attended my local mosque approached me. He asked me if I had heard the news. I replied "What news?" He mentioned that some Muslim kids had carried out suicide bombings in central London and that many people had died. He said that it was all over the news. I was shocked and perplexed. I wanted to know more and asked him a few questions but he himself could not comprehend what had happened and was unclear. I immediately went into a chip shop a few steps away which had a TV showing live coverage of the event. I was glued to the news in disbelief. The owner, a Kurdish Muslim, also expressed his disbelief and said something like "This is not good for the Muslims." I replied that "it was a day of sorrow for us."

I remember the rest of the day being dominated by media coverage trying to make sense of the event. One thing was clear: the mosques and Islamic organisations which were interviewed had one message in common; that Islam condemns 'terrorism' and the killing of innocent civilians, and they gave references from the Qur'an. However, I felt ashamed that it was Muslims who had perpetrated these acts and particularly as some of the bombers were educated and working in public sector jobs in this country. I was also worried about the impact it would have on Muslims in this country, as well as in other countries in Europe and across the Atlantic, especially after the repercussions of 9/11. In the next few days and weeks the discussions that took place among my Muslim friends and acquaintances expressed the same anxieties and sentiments as me. Many of them adopted a clear stance in condemning the 7/7 atrocities and liaising with the police in fear of their personal safety from what they thought the general public might do in retaliation.

I personally was not worried about myself or the Muslims in my community as we lived in a tolerant multicultural area. And until today, I am fortunate to say that I have not yet received any backlash or discrimination as a result of 7/7. This is despite me clearly expressing my religious identity by keeping a full beard and wearing religious attire when in public. The Muslim women in my community wearing the veil or the hijab were more apprehensive about walking in the streets during the early days after the event due to their fear of being insulted. However, again fortunately, this did not occur and they resumed their lives as before.

In the following weeks, as theories began to emerge as to the underlying cause of why these young Muslim males, who were born and bred in Britain, committed the atrocious acts, the government began to draw up ideas to integrate young Muslims into mainstream society. In my opinion, the notion they had were that mosques were not doing enough to educate the so called young breed of Muslim 'fundamentalists' who held extreme and anti-authoritarian views. Definitely, in my local mosques this was not the case, as the Muslims who worshiped there were labourers holding moderate religious views. Most of the Muslims in my area were not affluent and merely lived hand to mouth. However, ever since the event I have been summoned from time to time to participate in discussions with the police and other religious members from different faiths to promote peace and community cohesion.

Although in my community there has been no religious disharmony, these discussions nevertheless did make us feel safer and closer to each other. It also taught us practically how to prepare if another major incident such as 7/7 occurred in the future.

As for other Muslim communities in the UK, I know that in the aftermath of 7/7 they suffered violent retaliation and the police were deployed to protect mosques. During this time many Sikhs, especially in the Midlands, were also targeted as terrorists as some people mistook them as Muslims due to their beards and turbans. Both the retaliation and, evidently, the 7/7 attack heightened security everywhere. We now live in a 'big brother' state with CCTV cameras everywhere, including inside mosques.

Looking 5 years onwards, life is the same for me in Hackney. I still do not feel discriminated against or threatened due to my religious identity. It appears to me this is also the experience of other Muslims in Hackney. Nonetheless, as a Muslim I sometimes feel that, when the IRA terrorist activities took place in London in the 1990s, the government seemed less eager to suspect Irish people of being 'terrorists' than they have been with Muslims in the aftermath of 7/7. Also terrorism was less on the top of the agenda of government polices than it has been since 7/7. Why I ask myself? The former concern may be something to do with the fact that the appearance of Irish people may be less stereotyped than that of Muslims, who can be much easier to distinguish.

In terms of the government's policies on 'terrorism', I do not think they know what 'terrorism' is all about and how to deal with it effectively. Yes, they have taken countless security measures which are having an adverse effect on all walks of society, perhaps more so on Muslims, such as the excessive airport security checks. Whilst security measures may protect society from the aftermath of violent attacks, they do not eliminate the desire of individuals or groups to carry out such violent acts. The government has also taken countless measures to integrate young Muslims into mainstream society. But what does this 'integration' mean? Would their schemes and guidelines on 'citizenship' in schools and elsewhere help Muslims integrate? Would it mean Muslims should sacrifice their religious appearance, culture and practice in order to receive equal rights, for example, in unemployment, and to integrate? That goes on for me to question whether democracy in its entirety really exists in the UK? Can Muslims really practice their beliefs in the UK and do they really have freedom of speech? I believe these questions are in the forefront of many Muslim's minds.

I do believe that the integration of Muslims into mainstream society is an imperative need in understanding and dealing with young Muslims' grievances, which may otherwise lead them to adopt extremist views and reject the values of British multicultural society. For this, there needs to be more dialogue between these young Muslims and the main political parties and these interactions also need to be broadcast in the media. They must also be given opportunities themselves to play important roles in both the media and mainstream politics. At the same time, I also think Muslims have a significant role and need to take responsibility themselves to ensure that they do integrate with the general public in order to dispel misperceptions of Muslims as terrorists (and thus making it easier for the general public to integrate with them) in a way where they are not sacrificing their identity as Muslims.

No democratic country is without faults in its political system, but in my opinion the UK gives people from all walks of life enough opportunity and freedom to express their grievances without fear. It also provides them with ample opportunities to make a change. But many Muslims do not appreciate these freedoms and opportunities that they have or use them in the appropriate way to better their lives. Even the welfare system, which at times many Muslims are dependent on, does not discriminate against them.

On the whole Muslims will be treated differently, particularly if they see themselves as different. It is expected that people will have prejudices or stereotypes about a certain class or group of people, especially if they have been associated with certain atrocious events. But I do not think events such as 7/7 or 9/11 are principally responsible for these prejudices developing. It is more about how we as Muslims live and conduct ourselves as citizens of the United Kingdom. Often, when I start speaking to the general public, who may have certain misperceptions about me, they have responded with the comment "He's one of us".

THE 7/7 EFFECT

FATIMA KHAN

Fatima Khan is a freelance consultant with a wide range of experience engaging with communities on issues of safety and crime reduction. She is the Vice Chair of the Muslim Safety Forum (MSF), a charity focusing on issues of security and safety affecting the Muslim community; she also co-leads the MSF's Islamophobia work strand.

I CAN still remember exactly what I was doing when the story broke of the London bombings on the morning of 7th July 2005. I was at home, recovering from the flu. I woke up to see my husband leaving for work and settled in front of the television with a cup of tea. The news of the bombs broke very shortly afterwards. I thought initially that I did not understand properly what the reporters were saying, it took a good few minutes to internalise the information before I started to panic and call my husband, brothers and sisters and friends and family who take the Underground to work to find out their whereabouts. It took several phone calls before my husband picked up the phone; his office was located a short walk away from Aldgate tube station. Thankfully I managed to get through to all my loved ones and everyone confirmed they were safe. Many had a long walk home through the chaos in central London.

That morning I was also waiting for a repair man to come round and fix my heating. I realised this wouldn't happen now and thought it best to ring up the repair service and cancel the appointment. On getting through to the call centre, even before I managed to complete my sentence I was very rudely interrupted by the person on the other end of the line shouting 'there is a serious incident in London today if you hadn't noticed so what do you think!?' I was a little taken aback by this outburst and calmly informed the person that I had and was just ringing out of courtesy to cancel and then I put my phone down. A few seconds later my phone rang and to my surprise the same person had called me back to berate me for hanging up the phone and how they were not surprised really at my behaviour. I detected an undertone to all the shouting and asked to be transferred to the manager; this was not going to be so, again, I hung up and switched off my landline. Soon after, my husband walked in and I tried to put the phone conversations out of my mind, but a niggling feeling was telling me that things had changed in London.

The summer of 2005 I was working part time in central London, very close to Tottenham Court Road. I rescheduled my working days as I was a little nervous travelling on the tubes, especially as many of my friends described some not so very pleasant incidents to and from work. When I did eventually decide to brave it, I was nervous but luckily, apart from a few stares and some muttering, it wasn't too bad. I know it may seem that I was too aware, and in all likelihood I was looking into things too much, but I do believe that I am generally quite aware of my surroundings when I'm out and about. Life after 7/7 for someone visibly Muslim would mean getting used to some general unpleasantness, if only for a little while.

Just to give some background, when 9/11 took place I was in Egypt, travelling with a friend. I didn't wear a hijab at the time and had not experienced any problems arriving in Cairo via Paris. A week later, travelling home was an entirely different experience. Cairo airport was completely manic but we managed to just about board a plane going to Paris and were told to expect further delays in Paris. On arrival in Paris, we had to go through security checks. My friend was ahead of me in the queue and went through the checks quite smoothly. I, on the other hand, was stopped as the photo on my passport apparently had blue eyes and I clearly did not. I pointed out the jumper I was wearing in the passport was blue, not my eyes. The customs official shot me a dirty look, asked me to stand on the side. All the while, my friend had continued walking and talking to herself, not realising I was not by her side. She did eventually figure this out and walked back to find out what was happening. Meanwhile four other officials joined the officer who had pulled me aside. They brought out what I can only describe as a magnifying glass and kept looking through it at my picture and then at me. This went on for several minutes. They then had a conversation in French, looked at me disdainfully and then one abruptly waved his hand about as to say "now go away." So I did.

I did think then, "I wonder what it would be like if I wore a hijab" and prayed that I got home soon before my parents banned me from ever travelling again. I was in fact banned from travelling by my parents. The ban lasted a whole six months and I found out a few years later what it would be like to travel wearing a hijab.

Travelling aside, living in London seemed to be what everyone had to adjust to. It all seemed tense, like we were all waiting for something else to happen. The shooting of Jean Charles de Menezes had many on edge. For months, I was nervous every time my husband went out and probably irritated him to no end by calling him constantly.

In April 2006, I saw an advert for the role of Development Manager with an organisation called the Muslim Safety Forum (MSF). I didn't have all the experience they were asking for and the salary was quite low but it seemed like a fascinating role with a real learning opportunity. I was really thrilled when I was offered the position. Four years on, I am still very much involved with the Muslim Safety Forum, only now as a trustee.

It has been a rollercoaster journey to say the least. On my first day I was told to make sure I had some ID as I would be attending a meeting in New Scotland Yard with Muslim community leaders and senior police officers. It was literally a few days after the Forest Gate incident had taken place. I felt like I was completely in over my head and wanted to resign a few weeks into the job as I thought I would do a complete injustice to the role; the decent thing to do would be to say "I'm sorry, you need someone different for the role." However, I am really pleased I did not end up leaving. I was convinced to give it a few more weeks, which became two years.

Working with senior police and government officials was certainly an eye opening experience, not to mention working with the heads of leading Muslim organisations. It took me several months to get to grips with the role and to find how I really wanted to fit into all of this. One commonality I felt the Muslim groups shared with the police was that it seemed a very heavily male dominated arena where I often felt I was present to provide tokenistic value. At the same time I understood that in order to be counted I would have to work that much harder and not be over-sensitive.

The hours were very long, involved weekend work and the workload was extremely heavy. What kept me going was knowing that many of the individuals I worked with were extremely passionate about the work of the MSF and put in numerous unpaid hours daily. It felt really good to be part of something that I believed could make a genuine difference to people's lives. My own experiences since starting to wear a hijab sparked my interest in learning more about Islamophobia and anti-Muslim hate crime. The MSF provided me with the platform to understand how hate crimes are recorded, how they are misunderstood by both the police and the community and just how much work needed to be done in this area. Many of the projects I went on to design were shaped by what I understood to be the needs of the community from listening to the community.

My own personal experiences of Islamophobia may well be of a somewhat low level. But these reactions having being sustained over a period of time have made me feel at times far more vulnerable than I ever felt before I wore a hijab. Interestingly enough all the incidents took place after 7/7 but perhaps that was a coincidence, although more than likely it was not. In terms of the actual experiences, the perpetrators have always been men, either 'builder types' in a van shouting out profanities that have the word 'Muslim' in there somewhere, or they have been white men of eastern European origin who have been far more intimidating and aggressive. I have also noticed a trend of attracting a lot of unwanted attention if I dress in traditional Islamic clothes, for example, the jilbab, especially in black. I had on one occasion reported an incident online to the police and got absolutely no response back. Two weeks later I reported my mobile phone stolen and again used the online form and received a letter from the police with a crime reference number and a few days later a letter came through from Victim Support asking if I needed any support following my unfortunate experience. The experience they were referring to was the stolen phone!

My choice to start wearing a hijab in my mid-twenties was not related to 7/7 or any other world event. It was a personal choice a long time in the coming and very much part of a personal journey. The first year of wearing a hijab had its ups and downs, I had to give up my quarterly visits to Vidal Sassoon for a start, but thankfully I found a suitable alternative and did not settle for an auntie in a backstreet salon with garden shears for scissors! All the reasons I had for not wearing a hijab were actually not hard to adjust to or overcome. All these years later I sometimes find it hard to imagine a time I didn't wear a hijab. I did however lose some friends on this journey or perhaps they were never really friends to begin with. Either way, I look at them as people who were meant to be part of my life for a short while. In any case knowing what I know now, I wouldn't change a thing.

Going back to travelling after 7/7, now I was no longer travelling with friends or at least not simply friends, I would be travelling with my husband. I never have had any objections to being stopped and searched in customs, only to the manner in which the stopping, searching and questioning is done. Travelling out of the country has always been relatively smooth, travelling back is more eventful. My husband would be stopped nearly every time we returned to the UK, if only for a few minutes. I know this to be nothing compared to the experiences of friends and family and especially compared to the reports we had coming through to the MSF. Nonetheless, if compared with the law of averages I felt we were getting more than our fair share of random stops and questioning.

Growing up in London, I never really experienced the racism my elder siblings and parents had faced in the seventies and eighties as I was very young at the time. Apart from being called 'Paki' the odd few times here and there, I can honestly say that I only really became aware of my colour and what my faith meant to others after 7/7. Things had changed and the changes had a direct impact on the day to day lives of Muslims, however subtle. I needed to understand what this meant for me, my friends and family and how I can engage in the process, but better still work to change policies and processes that I felt were not working and were not in the interest of the community as a whole. At this moment in time I am still working towards that end.

The Terror of the Deserts

Ibrahim Lawson

Ibrahim Lawson spent several years as a young man travelling and studying esoteric spiritual traditions before settling in Norfolk and accepting Islam under the guidance of a teaching Shaykh. Following a degree in Philosophy, he trained as a teacher of religious studies at Cambridge University and spent 10 years working in state education. During this time he studied for a Masters course in Phenomenological Research and, later, in Theology. He set up his first school in 1999 and three years later was seconded to the National College for School Leadership while beginning a PhD in Radical Hermeneutics. He is currently the Head Teacher of an Islamic secondary school in London.

JULY 7th two thousand and something. I was in the back seat of a minivan, two Indians up front; a hot night. We were driving back to my empty villa on the seafront in Sharjah leaving behind us Maha Lal's supermarket just across the border into Ajman. My shopping was in the back – a free delivery plus a lift. No car yet – I was trying to buy something but the right deal hadn't come up. The radio was playing; something in rapid Malayalam segued into the news. "London... London... Terrorists... police..." What? The guys said there had been a bomb going off in London. Right.

We get back down to the seafront and they bring the bags into the air-conditioning for me. The place really is empty; marble floors, four bedrooms, three bathrooms, two living rooms and not a stick of furniture or any other person except me. It was really hot under the too bright fluorescent lights in the kitchen. Alone again in the night. Empty.

What is surprising in retrospect is that I didn't really have any feelings left. I had been angry before, especially when the Second Gulf war started. Shock and Awe. Fuck 'em all! Blow up the whole fucking city, why not? 10 years of murderous sanctions; 500,000 children dead. Why not just go the whole genocidal 10,000 yards and bomb them back into the Stone Age?

By 2005, I had had enough of all of 'them' actually. All the madness, the suicide bombings, the lying, the hypocrisy, the sheer, vicious deceit on all sides. Who was right or wrong anymore? No one knew anything. It was a world run by the worst kind of deluded idiots at best. How can anyone who has no connection to the Real make any kind of informed choices? So I left it all behind and headed east.

What was different about living in the Gulf was the lack of Eurocentric focus. I mean, I wasn't in Dubai; I wasn't connected to any European world at all. I liked being in Sharjah: there was no alcohol. The focus was east, not west. I didn't know anyone who wasn't Muslim. So the perception was different. Fallujah was way closer than London. Iran was just out of view; over the horizon, but not by much and India was ever-present.

7/7. I knew it would happen. In 2003 I had written a piece for the National College of School Leadership about two young men from Derby who went to Israel to do something violent; one was found dead, I can't remember what happened to the other one. They were born in the UK and went to school for at least 11 years by law; another few by choice. How many more like them were sitting in classrooms around the country, on a trajectory towards some act of explosive nihilism? Did any head teachers out there ever worry about that? How did a boy survive 11 plus years of British state education and end up thinking that blowing himself up with as many incidental bystanders as possible was a positive contribution to society in any way whatsoever?

So I wasn't surprised, I wasn't shocked, I was…. resigned. I had resigned. I didn't want to know any more. I was NEVER going back to the UK anyway. Wherever I went next, it would not be the West. Never again. For 25 years, since I dropped back in the UK, but this time as a Muslim, I had been deluding myself into thinking change was possible. That someone would listen. That human nature was essentially rational and good. Bullshit!

I blame the 60's, personally. One of my first conscious memories (I was maybe 5) is walking upstairs to our flat in Russell Square holding my dad's hand and wondering not if, but when, they dropped the bomb on London and a wall of fire came rushing down the stairs towards me. I could see it coming, wondering if it would hurt. Or would it be over so quickly? I think I ceased to have any long-term expectations from an early age.

We lived in Bloomsbury, in the flat my grandparents had lived in when my dad was a boy. A top floor tenement. We went to Regent's Park for a treat, or Hampstead Heath. One of the bombs went off in Southampton Row. I could have been there. Later, I lived round the corner in Burton Street; we all had a squat there in the late 70's, where my first child was born. I had a restaurant in a local art gallery; we could have been there when the bombs went. Before moving to the Emirates, I was working in Aldgate. My dad worked at number 1 Watling Street – the Roman road that goes to Scotland. My granddad worked at the Bank of England. But who was I?

Recently, I have been surprised to realise that I am a Londoner, like my father and grandfather. Not just a Londoner, but a Muslim from Bloomsbury. So I am at that space-time crossroads where the bombs went off. I AM that crossroads. This gives me something to say about all of this.

I was an OFSTED inspector for a while. They wanted me to help with inspection of Islamic schools. One madrasah I did was up north. I feel right at home; I know this environment and they know me. For several years I was invited round mosques in the Midlands and North to give talks in English. I taught Pakistani teenagers for years in Nottingham – 10 miles from Derby. I led the prayer in the local mosque when hardly anyone turned up for 'Isha' on a late summer night. I set up the local Islamic school.

Who, then, is this 'gora' in a suit? Who likes a nap on the floor of the mosque after the midday prayer, much to the 'mawlanas'' approval? Who tears off to Luton afterwards, to Easyjet, down to Nice where his wife is waiting with supper on the table in a little flat just up behind the Russian Cathedral with orange trees in the garden?

On the plane, I am re-reading 'The Social Construction of Reality' when a line leaps out: 'What conditions thought?'

Where do people get their ideas from? Where does a thought come from? Where is it before it is thought?

Or: where is all this crap coming from?

I remember being young and revelling in the fact that I was socially excluded. In fact, I was the one who had done the excluding. Me and millions of others it seemed. My friends in Paris were hosting a revolution; the Stones played for free in the park; Grace Slick was singing: 'We are forces of chaos and anarchy. All that they say we are, we are, we are. And we are very proud of ourselves.' The Dead tripped gratefully through the transitive nightfall of diamonds.

The orient drew us in; smoking black hashish on top of the Buddhas in Bamiyan we found some answers and even more questions. It was clear that the West was finished but that the human soul was eternal. We had to get back to the source.

I did come back from the Emirates briefly in the July of 2005. I was towing an oversized Sony hi-fi system on a trolley I had had to buy specially for the job; it was far too big really. A present for my brother. He has lived and will live in a small stone village up a mountain in the Languedoc, in the middle of the biggest vineyard in Europe; he gave up years ago, becoming a blue grass musician and luthier. He needed a new stereo.

I got onto the train at Gatwick dragging the monster on its trolley and a suitcase. England was weirdly cold even in summer after three months in the sauna that is the Arabian Gulf coast. I felt free, like when I left school and just went back briefly to collect my stuff and drop off some text books, I didn't belong here anymore among these green and pleasant fields among all these white people.

The last thirty years had been a 'long strange trip'. After living for a year on a Gurdjieff (look it up) community in the blue ridge mountains of West Virginia, I suddenly found myself the father of another soul who had somehow chosen me to look after him: Daniel James, soon to be Umar Abdul Quddus ibn Ibrahim Lawson. Moving from Bloomsbury to Norwich. Finding that further out than the most extreme edge of turn on, tune in, drop-out, anarchist radicalism there was, amazingly, Sufism. It was like stumbling blind, drunk and alone through the night time ruins of a city with the rain pouring down, down and the clouds so low and the wind roaring and moaning to suddenly open a door into a sunlit garden of trees and lawns with people like myself smiling welcome, glad you could make it.

But the thing was, we had to go back. It's not enough to turn your back on the world; it's not even possible except as another fantasy. The Real demands no less than total commitment; the inward IS the outward and the outward IS the inward. One hand cannot clap by itself. In short – there is no spirituality without politics.

So I returned to the world. There I found again that there was something fundamentally wrong; but I was beginning to understand what that might be. One of my earliest coherent thoughts that I can remember was that something had to be wrong with society – that is, the people around me. Whatever it was, it was at a level so fundamental as to be invisible. What foundational assumption were people making that was not only completely false but that we didn't even have the means to detect or that we had no way of suspecting?

I understand now that it is an element so implicit in European thinking that it cannot even be described. It cannot be grasped because to grasp it is to have grasped it already so as to leave no trace, no further object of inquiry.

I know, that's just confused. Try this – "For manifestly you have long been aware of what you mean when you use the expression 'being'. We, however, who used to think we understood it, have now become perplexed." With this quotation from Plato, Heidegger begins his most substantial early work, 'Being and Time'. He goes on to propose that we have completely forgotten the question of the meaning of being, forgotten that there even is such a question. And with this we are off on a completely new start in western thinking; or perhaps a re-appropriation of its most original genius among the pre-Socratics. Cutting to the mid 1950's, Heidegger is able to say, "The most extreme sharpness and depth of thought belongs to the genuine and great mystics." 'Thought' here being contrasted with 'philosophy' as a more profound mode of cognition than the latter.

So we are nearly there. Meanwhile, I am sitting on a crowded train rattling through the countryside north to London on a summer's morning in 2005 and there's a young Muslim male, cropped hair, long beard, shalwar kameez... am I the only one who's suddenly very nervous? Is he carrying a rucksack? Am I worrying about the forgetting of the question of the meaning of being? Or getting my legs blown off at the knees?

Flashback to Colchester, 1974. The IRA had taken to bombing pubs frequented by soldiers. It was the first time I'd heard the word 'anti-personnel' to describe a bomb designed to inflict maximum damage, not on property but on human bodies. I was spending the evening in just such a pub. In fact, wait a minute, anyone my age will remember the IRA campaigns; we've felt that fear of the random stranger before. Where was the 'war on terror' then?

But the Irish hadn't been keen on taking themselves along on the ride to oblivion. They stopped just short of that. Same attitude though. The same attitude that runs through all terrorist fantasies and banking ideologies: nothing is true; everything is permitted. God is dead and we have killed Him. Nihilism.

When Nietzsche announced the death of metaphysics, he declared the inevitable demise of Platonic thought (Socrates having wisely left nothing so concrete). Philosophy was freed to recover its roots in the thinking of Being. The world paid little attention. Nietzsche went mad in despair. Heidegger described the new world in 'The Question Concerning Technology'; unauthenticity grew to new heights; wars passed and the second industrial revolution loomed; an anarchist actor turned playwright journeyed to Morocco and wrote 'The Book of Strangers'.

In the end, there was no escape. I had not understood the past and was condemned to repeat it. Thirty five years after discovering that Islam was the key to every door and, letting myself in, being surprised to find my new brothers letting themselves out through the same door to the very place I was relieved to be leaving. Metaphysical thinking. It never worked. It was obviously never going to, possibly even to Plato in the end. Over the next 2 millennia plus, the mind falls into the world and then cannot find itself. Despair follows and turns inwards. I have nothing to lose because I am nothing; but if I annihilate my nothingness perhaps my life might mean something after all.

This is the extreme condition. Most of us in the West are enabled to believe that things can't be all that bad because we have, after all, a relatively comfortable material existence. That 20 or 30,000 children per day die somewhere in the world from entirely preventable causes is not seen as directly connected with this marvellous ability to delude ourselves that life is really OK and that, in any case, there is nothing we can do about it.

So I was dragged back, by Allah, to the last place I wanted to be ever again. I was reminded of a slogan I was once amused by: 'Wrong place, wrong time. Be there!' And of course, that is exactly right; that is where Being reveals itself most readily for questioning. And I drag myself back to this: how can we educate ourselves and our children to know who we really are and to know that we have the choice to define ourselves and our worlds as the greatest and most perfect of Allah's creations?

THE ALARM BELL

ASRA FAREED

Asra Fareed was born in India. She works as a Corporate Communications Manager at a cable company in Amsterdam where she has lived with her husband since December 2006. Previously she worked in London as a PR Manager at an advertising agency working in multicultural marketing communications.

A S the morning alarm on my mobile phone went off at 7.00hrs, I buried my head in the pillow and switched the mobile off. An hour and 45 minutes later, I was dashing to the bus stop to catch the number 29 to Manor House tube station. I was so late for work. The bus stop was buzzing and seemed unusually crowded. I wasn't sure if that was how busy it usually was at that hour. Bus 29 arrived but I stood no chance. There were at least 30 people before me! I pulled out my phone to call work, and that is when I realised something was wrong, very wrong. I recall seeing 20 missed calls and many more text messages enquiring about my well being.

The July 2005 London bombings altered my perspective on terrorism and life. Things that happened to others were suddenly up-close and personal.

My reaction to the unfortunate incidents went through different phases and levels. My initial reaction as a regular Londoner was of guilt, anger and frustration followed by insecurity, fear, suspicion, and empathy. I battled feelings of guilt – guilt by association because I am Muslim and Muslims were the likely suspects in this case. To be associated by faith with people who may be behind this unjustifiable bloodbath was most perplexing. I was angry with the perpetrators for making things worse for the Muslim population in general, adding to the increased unpopularity and negative image of Islam. In the following days and weeks, I grew increasingly frustrated as my 30 minutes commute to work had turned into a daily two-hour nightmare.

Coming from New Delhi, the control centre for a billion plus population, I had often been awed by the London Underground; how painless and convenient it was to commute from one end of the city to the other; a stark contrast to the chaotic commuting scene in New Delhi. That changed. I was wary of the Underground and did at one point ask myself if I had given the tube a 'bad nazar' (evil eye)! Now with each tube ride, my mind went on a rather wild imagination trip. I imagined different scenarios on how I would react if there were a bomb blast two coaches down. Of course, even in my thoughts the bomb never went off in my coach as firstly, I was too scared to even imagine that and, secondly, somehow things still happened to others!

The London bombings brought me an inch closer to the suffering of people living in conflict-affected parts of the world. I experienced a bit of what it meant living in fear. I could now at least attempt to relate to the anxiety, mental agony and insecurity that a Palestinian, Afghan, Iraqi or a Kashmiri would experience each day of his life. It was honestly nerve racking. I learned to empathize better.

On another level, gripped by fear, I recall changing coaches when I saw 'suspicious' people on the tube. Embarrassingly enough, I must admit now that I was constantly looking out for the 'usual suspects'. I was suddenly suspicious of my modest sisters who covered their heads and wore long flowing gowns, of my brothers who sported beards and carried backpacks. I was increasingly scrutinizing 18-40 years old Muslim men and women of South Asian and African origin; regular people who just like me were equally perturbed by the state of affairs. I guess I may have made a lot of them rather uncomfortable with my unusually long stares. Some paid me back in the same coin while some simply added to the anxiety by rummaging through their bags, and finally pulling out a book or an apple. In other words, my mind was constantly feeding on the media frenzy, and I was getting paranoid to the extent that even now I believe that I saw one of the 21st July bombers on the tube a day before his unsuccessful attempt.

As I managed to wean myself off the suspicion, I started taking note of how the media covered the bombings and the political reaction to the incidents. While the BBC was being accused of being overtly conscious of British Muslim sentiments and of 'sanitizing' its coverage, by not referring to the London bombers as 'terrorists' but simply as 'bombers', the tabloids' headlines and articles smacked of Islamophobic, unwarranted and negative portrayals of Muslims. In 2001, during my Master's studies in London, I had analyzed the role of the local vernacular press in the 2002 anti-Muslim pogroms in Gujarat, India, and the conclusions recorded that the Gujarati vernacular press was guilty of aggravating tensions, inciting violence and reprisal attacks through inflammatory coverage. I could now draw clear parallels.

On the other hand, when comparing 07/07 to 09/11, I also realized that much of the political hysteria in the UK was amiss. I guess there were not enough buyers for that type of sentiment. The British public was well aware of their government's role in Iraq and Afghanistan, and perhaps in a way expected some form of retaliation. Ken Livingstone, the Mayor of London, had earlier appealed to Tony Blair not to support the war in Iraq, saying, "An assault on Iraq will inflame world opinion and jeopardize security and peace everywhere. London, as one of the major world cities, has a great deal to lose from war and a lot to gain from peace, international cooperation and global stability."

I was also seeking answers to bigger questions. What would be the long term effects of the bombings? How would this impact the Muslim population in the UK and the rest of the world? And most importantly, the why of the what – why was London bombed?

At the given time, the long-term effects could only be speculative, but over time they seem to have come true. The attack made it more politically viable to continue indefinitely the 'War on Terror' which many Muslims understood as 'War on Islam'. It further helped the involved governments to justify and continue the occupation of Iraq, and may perhaps, in the near future, justify the invasion of Iran as well.

The impact on the Muslim population was obvious very soon, with the subsequent reprisal attacks. My friends wearing headscarves were attacked and had passers-by shout abuse at them. I recall my close friend breaking down over the uncomfortable glances she got on buses and trains. She decided to 'down size' her bag to attract lesser attention. The other, born of a white English father and a Moroccan mother, had a bunch of neighbourhood hooligans attack her in Camden. They pulled off her headscarf, punched her in the face and yes, 'asked her to go back to where she came from'. Two of my other friends of Bangladeshi origin also received a similar message from a drunken woman on bus 168 to Holborn. In my opinion, the worst victims of the London bombings were British Muslims. I did not wish to be in their shoes. Their identity was split into two. They were suddenly British and Muslim and struggling hard to harmonize their split identity. They were perceived as a threat to their own country and to the British 'mainstream' way of life. Tony Blair confirmed this by blaming the bombings on the attackers' "hatred for our way of life and values." Did the bombers blow themselves and tens of people up simply to protest against fish and chips, bars, restaurants and other aspects of lifestyle?

The 'Why' of the bombing was rather obvious. It had little to do with my 'bad nazar' or an attempt to 'change the British life' and more to do with the Palestinian's suffering, and the involvement of the British government in the Afghanistan and Iraq wars. The oppression of the Palestinians over the last decades has undoubtedly angered the world's Muslims, as did the first Iraq war and the sanctions against Iraq which resulted in the deaths of half a million children, described as 'a price worth paying' by Madeline Albright, the then US Secretary of State. According to the four suicide bombers, Britons needed a bitter taste of their own medicine. The British public was being punished for choosing a government that supported Israel, a government that led to the war in Afghanistan and Iraq. Britons were being punished for believing the Anglo-American whipped-up hysteria around the notion of weapons of mass destruction, and for the death and suffering inflicted upon hundreds and thousands of innocent men, women and children in the Muslim world. Their argument was perhaps sane, but their actions were certainly not. Two wrongs can never make a right. Understanding the causes of violence does not mean condoning it. It is the sensible response to find a solution to a grave problem. In fact the majority of Muslims have condemned the bombings and would agree that the incidents have made things lot worse for them and added to the demonisation of Islam and its fundamentals.

The media and the terrorists can, out of context, misquote verses from the Holy Qur'an. I know Islam does not sanction killing innocent people, period. I can defend Islam till I turn blue in my face, but there is also no denying that the actions of few individuals, with their perverted understanding of the religion, have reflected negatively on the larger community as a whole. This places a duty on Muslims, particularly in Britain, to contribute to the debate to understand and stop such acts. It also places a duty on the British government, community organisations and the media to ensure that the British Muslims are not made to stand trial for atrocities committed by Muslim individuals whether in Britain or anywhere else in the world.

Us, Them, & 'Them'

Mohammad Sartawi

Mohammad Sartawi is a Palestinian-Kuwaiti. He is a doctoral candidate in Social Psychology at the London School of Economics. His thesis is concerned with the everyday experience and practice of Islam in London's Muslim communities. More specifically he is interested in the relationship between beliefs, identity, and different forms of practice in different Islamic groups in a Western context. His interests include social identity theory, social representations, phenomenological epistemologies, and social/collective action. He is the Coordinator of the LSE Social Representations Group and a member of the Social Psychological Research into Racism and Multiculturalism group at the LSE Institute of Social Psychology.

A S I stood shoulder to shoulder with the men on my left and right, the smells of the scented oils they wore filled my head with memories of home. The sun shone through the blue-tinted circular windows that lined the base of the dome above and scattered streams of tranquil colours all around us. I heard the play and laughter of children just outside, some sounding naughty, others nice. All around the building a host of birds sang, chirped, and chattered, filling the hall with the sounds of August in the park. In stark contrast, the hall where we stood was as still as silence, and nothing louder than a whisper emerged from its hundred or so occupants. There couldn't have been a more peaceful place to be in the city. This was our sanctuary from the madness of the world outside. We all stood patiently waiting for the prayer to commence.

This has now become a place where I belong. I had a job to do here, and people came to me to get things done. The imams were my friends and the regular attendees my brothers, and I had an office with a desk and my own extension number. I had my daily morning commute here, and had made that trip enough times to know all the alternatives in case one of the buses happened not to be running on a given day. I bought my morning coffee from the shop in the basement and drank it with the maintenance workers behind the mosque where we could hide our cigarette smoke and compare cultural habits, traditional dishes, and linguistic dialects. Things would sometimes even get heated; who grew better olives? Where was the superior quality of fish to be found? Who had better weather? I would then assume my position at the desk I was assigned where I would remain for most of the day to come. Indeed this mosque has now become a place where I belong. This, however, was not the case not so long ago.

Then, I did not know the men who stood beside me. They were my brothers nevertheless, and together we formed the lines that made our prayers more beneficial to all of us. As soon as the prayers were completed we all went our own ways. I would not recognize these men if I saw them again. I stood by such men several times every day, and although we had shared one of the most intimate and personal experiences a person could have, they remained perfect strangers to me. In fact, if one of them approached me I would be suspicious of his motives, cautious and guarded as to how much of myself I revealed, or to what lengths I would go to assist them or meet their requests. 'Brothers' by label and nothing more. This was our present reality, despite our ideals that were now, more than ever, stories from the past, tales, and fantasies.

We all remember exactly where we were when we first heard the news. I was about to complete the final phase of data collection before writing up my Master's dissertation at the University of Dundee, Scotland. My trip to London was planned for the following week where I would distribute my questionnaires and hope to have more luck with respondents than I had had in Scotland. I loved coming to London, and had heard about it all my life, as far back as I can remember. Having been raised in Kuwait, most of the people I knew, including friends and close relatives, had been coming here all their lives. My mother made her first trip here with her family as a teenager, and then made several repeat visits since. It is one of the oldest and grandest capitals of Western Europe and perhaps the most culturally mixed and diverse in the world. Everyone could fit in London, and no one could be too different to be different. This was all about to change.

My flat-mate called me into the living room to see what was being reported on the news. As I approached the television I was in disbelief as to what I saw. It took a few minutes for me to absorb what was being said. I was horrified. The first thing that came to mind was whether or not any of the many friends and relatives I had in the city was affected. I immediately got on the phone and began calling everyone I knew who lived in or was visiting the capital. When I was done I experienced little relief from the anxiety and dread that I was feeling; the dread one feels when reminded of how much hate and violence the world can produce. Not even the power and might of the developed world could prevent such things from happening. Nowhere could we be safe. My flat-mate urged me not to follow through with my plans, and to stay in Scotland – at least until things more or less settled. I could not deviate from my plans, however. I had a deadline to meet. I began worrying about using public transport, about the monsters that lurked in the shadows underground or on the buses. I then began to fear the wrath of those affected for whom my skin tone or facial hair made me a monster. Would they take the time to see past my brown skin? Would they try to understand me before I was judged by my beard?

Being an optimist to a fault, almost naive even, I made preparations to leave a few days later. We had been glued to the television screen and our heads were full of news reports, updates, and warnings. I took solace in the fact that the tightened security and screening procedures would keep us safe from the monsters. But then who was to keep me safe from the new safety procedures? I placed my trust in the organization and efficiency of the powers of the developed world and took the train down to London. Aside from managing to collect the data I needed to complete my Masters, my trip was otherwise uneventful. I was not stopped or searched once in the 10 days I was in the capital despite the heavy police presence I encountered everywhere I went.

Fate and circumstance conspired to bring me to the capital once again, this time as a resident, not a visitor. I accepted an offer at the London School of Economics for a doctoral candidacy in Social Psychology and moved to London five months after the 7/7 attacks. The extent of the impact the events would have only became clear to me once I moved to the city. The disbelief I experienced towards the growing anti-Islamic sentiment that was explicitly prevalent was even greater than that which I had when I first heard the news. It was perhaps less the sentiment than its expression. It was everywhere, on the television, in seminars, on the internet, and in people's eyes. It hurt. The religion that formed the foundations of everything I was raised with, morals, beliefs, and common decency was reviled and ridiculed publicly. This was the religion of my parents, our way of life, kindness and virtue, everything good; it was what my grandmother epitomized. If they knew what Islam meant to me, what it represented, surely they could not hate or fear it so much, could they?

I made it my mission to explore the world of London's Muslims and study the experience of the Muslim community. This was to become the subject of my doctoral thesis. I grew tired of the sensationalism that surrounded the topics of Islamism, terrorism, extremism and an entire host of other -isms that claimed to uncover the intricacies of the hatred and violence that emerged under the guise of Islam. I did not know Islam to be so, and the so-called Islam that these people studied was not the one that I was familiar with. I had heard stories about it, but only recently had it invaded my life and managed with its hatred to vilify me, my parents, and my grandmother as well. Now we were grouped together, so much so that we couldn't even tell each other apart by just looking. I feared the bearded man in a turban sitting next to me on the tube as much as he feared me. We saw each other not through the eyes of Muslims but through the eyes of Londoners. This was the picture that London had painted of him and me. I wanted to paint a new picture of Muslims in London in the colours of my Islam.

The first step in my study was to become part of the Muslim community in London. I had to be where they went and do what they did. I therefore sought out volunteer work in some of the largest mosques in the city. To my surprise, volunteering at a mosque was no longer as simple and straightforward as it once used to be. I always approached the key figures responsible for the overall running and management of the mosques. Continuing to observe research ethics I also always introduced myself as a doctoral researcher who was interested in the everyday experiences of London's Muslims. I would then offer to do any available work on a voluntary basis in order to be able to interact with members of the community and observe everyday practices. These requests came across as extremely strange to most, and were met with more than a little suspicion and distrust. In reading over my notes from those moments I could almost experience the uneasy tension that permeated my conversations with those men. In some cases it took me over three months to gain access and get a job, and this was after making several requests, appealing to different people in positions of authority, acquiring references from my department's director and doctoral supervisor, sending in resumes, and filling out several application forms. I can imagine it is not so different getting a job at the Ministry of Defence. And all this despite the fact that the mosques I worked for were all under-staffed and could not afford to pay wages for qualified people to work for them. In the end, however, perseverance prevailed.

I was only to understand the extent of the suspicion and distrust that now defines the Muslim community when I became part of it. 'Brothers' would not give me the time of day, and if they did I would wonder what they were after. We were almost afraid to help people if they asked us to. Many Muslims seemed to even fear their own beliefs which the media represented as 'extremist', 'fundamentalist' or, by those more inclined towards political correctness, as 'controversial'. They were weary of Muslims who saw them through the lens of the media, and those who wore the lens of the media were weary of them. They did not want to be associated with each other lest one community or the other may reject them. The mosques were no longer full of Muslims, but of this, that, or the other Muslim. Newcomers to London would often complain to me about the absence of our glorified brotherhood. "Where is our Ummah?" they would ask. I was often cautioned by the people I worked for not to trust so easily, to be suspicious, and to constantly question. I remember once that a man from Jordan who was stopping over in London for one night only came to the mosque one evening. He had a duffle bag that he needed to pass on to an old widowed woman who lived in Birmingham. Someone was driving down the following day to collect it. This man, however, needed to catch a flight and could not wait. Naturally, he thought, he could leave it with the brothers at the mosque until someone came to pick it up. None of us at the mosque would hold this bag for him. We were more eager to send him away than we were to help him. This is what has become of our brotherhood. 7/7 not only had us all pigeonholed as one and the same type of people, it also tore us apart from within.

During the years that I have been a researcher I kept close watch on the media and became involved in several projects that focused on how Muslims were represented. The terms 'witch-hunt' and McCarthyism came to define this experience for me. There was always an individual, group, or institution that was 'uncovered' or 'exposed'. The Muslims were everywhere, conspiring to take over with their veiled women, halal food and Sharia law. As long as they had Islamic beliefs and adhered to orthodox Islamic practices they were fair game. On more than one occasion I was acquainted with an individual or institution that was

121

'exposed' and experienced firsthand the extent of distortion and misrepresentation characteristic of many of the programs allowed to be broadcast here. The media do not discriminate. They vilify the good and the bad, the violent and the peaceful, the malignant and the benign. They feed the fury of the masses hurt by the events on 7/7 and direct it towards anything affiliated with the banner of 'Islam'. Now even their hate does not discriminate. One needs only to browse readers' comments on any news website following articles that report on issues surrounding Islam in the UK to experience the magnitude of this effect.

My work within London's Muslim community has brought me closer to the Islam that I believe in. I have rediscovered the religion of my childhood and come to love it all over again. I grew to love the mosques here and the people I worked with. They were the same people in the mosques at home. They were the faces that smiled, the hands that took mine with genuine warmth and interest, the eyes that noticed when I was absent. They became part of the Islam that filled my heart. However I no longer know if the Islam in my heart is the Islam out there in the world. I no longer know what the Islam out there in the mosques, on the streets, in the hearts of the men who stand on either side of me during prayer is. Nevertheless my Islam and theirs has caused me to be stopped and searched on the street, in the Underground, and in airports. The men I pray with are only brothers in some ideal that we hold, a past that is no longer. In reality they are unmemorable strangers who, for all I know, know nothing of the Islam of my childhood, the Islam in my heart. But since 7/7, we are one and the same nevertheless.

ON 'BECOMING' MUSLIM

SERENE KASIM

Serene Kasim works as Research Fellow with the Centre for the Study of Culture and Society (CSCS), Bangalore, India. She is part of an international project funded by Hivos in the Netherlands. It is a part of their Knowledge Programme and is called Promoting Pluralism in India. The project aims to study religious pluralism in multicultural societies and move towards an understanding of fundamentalisms. Serene has an MA in South Asian Area Studies from the School of Oriental and African Studies, University of London.

IDENTITY is a tenuous thing. How does one begin thinking of oneself? There are my likes and dislikes and a thousand quirks of personality that someone might identify as being uniquely me. But if we take this further and ask what makes me Muslim, what answer is there? How have recent events on the world stage affected the Muslim in me? How do I answer that? Did the events of the past decade or so make me think of myself as primarily Muslim? Were these events and their fall-out what precipitated the feeling of "I am not 'I' any longer but part of a collective 'we'?" When did that happen? Was there a specific incident or an event that brought about this change in self-perception? Did the headline proclaiming 'Muslim' terrorists bombing or maiming hundreds, suddenly lead to a defensiveness concerning the use of that specifically Muslim description of these criminals?

I was born into an Indian Muslim family from the state of Kerala. That was the closest I had ever come to thinking of myself as Muslim. It was never a badge of honour (or dishonour). The wearing of the hijab or the lack of one was never really an issue. Having had a thoroughly cosmopolitan upbringing in the Persian Gulf state of Oman, I had friends and acquaintances from every walk of life and every community and country imaginable within the expatriate community in that country. Perhaps the locals made distinctions between 'Muslim' Indians and 'Hindu' Indians. But it seemed to me some kind of quaint silliness on their part to have made that distinction. Perhaps all this is some trick of memory where the past is always golden and idyllic. Perhaps there were subtle signals that I missed or my younger self failed to process. Perhaps being Muslim was more than the fasting during Ramadan and the celebrations of Eid. But these questions were not of any particular concern for my family or me.

And then 9/11 happened and my world began to change – very slowly at first. There were little trickles of disquiet that I could never fully articulate. I was still in Oman when the twin towers were brought down. My geography insulated me from the more acute effects and reactions of that momentous event. A visit to the United States six months later passed off without event. I was still me. I seemed to be assessed simply at face value. Three years later in May of 2005, I went back and JFK airport had become a seemingly almost impenetrable fortress with the Department of Homeland Security flexing every well-armed muscle. I had my first experience of being singled out for my name, for my passport and for my country of embarkation; Oman. For the first time, I was being led away by the uniformed officials to a separate room with all eyes on me. It was brought home to me quite forcefully that I was in some way different from the thousands who had disembarked that day with me; that I was in some way worthy of suspicion of possible heinous crimes. I remember my first reaction as being what can only be described as a certain disdain. I also remember trying to rationalize their procedures; their way of trying to 'weed out' potential threats. There were others in that room; – an elderly South Asian couple, a seven year old boy – all of us waiting for something as yet not articulated in any particular way. A couple of hours and a few hundred questions later I was finally 'allowed' to go. Throughout that visit there were chance remarks or casual questions that always threw me off balance. When recounting the experiences with Homeland Security, along with the many expressions of sympathy there would also be a handful in any given room, who would say, "Well obviously, she's Muslim; she came in from the Middle East. Of course, they would question her. It's natural." My mother's reaction on the other hand was quite funny. Trying to reassure me she said, "Well, look at it this way, now they have all your information and they know you will not be packing any explosives under your clothes!" Don't take it to heart was her advice.

July of that year when the London bombings took place, I was still in New York. I sat in a friend's living room and watched in disbelief as pictures of the mangled bus in Tavistock Square and the dead and injured were flashed in high definition clarity on my host's television screen. Over the next few days as details of those who had committed the atrocity trickled in I found it hard to digest that such people could commit such acts. A few days later I was back in Oman and a month later I was in London to enrol at the School of Oriental and African Studies (SOAS).

London, unlike New York, was welcoming. The bustle of Heathrow felt almost like an Indian airport. Immigration was politely distant and refreshingly enough there was no singling out of individuals – at least none that I saw. The streets were even more open and welcoming. There was no 'Fortress London'. But then I remembered that six months after 9/11, New York was hardly the fortress that it had become in recent years. Londoners I met did not seem particularly concerned about threats, real or imagined. Yes, there were random checks in tube stations. But there were equally newspapers and student groups and civil liberties groups who raised a hue and cry against racial profiling. Headlines about 'Islamist terrorism' and 'Muslim terrorists' competed with headlines expressing outrage over the killing of an innocent Brazilian student following the 7/7 bombings. Debates were vocal and no opinion seemed to go unexpressed. However, personal thoughts of my 'Muslimness' took a back seat to the excitement of being a student in a campus as vibrant and multicultural as SOAS. The city itself was a revelation. It quickly felt like home.

And then, one fine day, in the course of a casual conversation about a year into my stint at SOAS, an acquaintance said to me, "I wouldn't like to be in your shoes right now – as a Muslim woman." Until that exact point in time, the various burka, torture and racial profiling debates were to me merely academic. These were things to be taken with a pinch of salt as the media making a mountain out of a mole hill. They were not things that affected me in any real way. Or so I had thought. But here was someone who I'd known a few months and who, with no apparent malice, simply stated what she was thinking. After New York, this was possibly only the second time that perceptions of me as a Muslim woman, were driven home to me in the most basic of ways – as a victim almost; as someone for whom certain doors would be harder to open. Whether this was in actual fact the truth or not, did not seem to matter to most. And this time, it stuck. If anyone were to ask me now, I can clearly point to this moment as that point of no return when the debates swirling around me became very much about me. I was forced to confront my 'Muslimness' finally.

It was not a happy confrontation. Having a mirror held up to oneself, a mirror that does not reflect one's image but a mirror that reflects someone else's image of that self, is not always a pleasant experience. In fact it can be very confusing to say the least. It is a moment that upsets one's equilibrium; one's self-perceived role in the grander scheme of things. An accident of birth had somehow ensured that I became a part of a debate that I had never felt (and still do not feel) a personal stake in. I have never worn a hijab and neither has my mother or any of the other women in my family. And yet, I felt compelled to stand up for those who chose to do so – not merely as a liberal who stands for everyone's right to choose what they wear and how they live their lives but also as a Muslim woman standing with others in her community.

I may not follow all the dictates of my religion and I may not even be what would fit most people's description of a 'good' Muslim, but somehow I had been branded as Muslim – whatever that meant to the people branding me. I once asked a Jewish friend, if it was possible that I was a self-hating Muslim? You see, my faith had always been a deeply private part of me. And here I was being forced into a box that I was not willing to be part of. The 'I' was being forced into a 'we'. I almost resented it. I resented the implications of the one extra security check at the airport. I resented the implications of a friend telling me that to a guy I wanted to date, my being Muslim might be a concern if he wasn't part of the community.

The constant debates around that little square piece of cloth and the constant debates around a loosely understood Sharia; the headlines that insist on branding those who are essentially thugs and criminals as 'Muslim' terrorists; the subtexts of conversations that hinted at "you're Muslim, you must have an opinion on this" – these were things that started to take a toll and began to rankle.

My personal confusion and my 'crisis of faith' led me down an academic path that I had hardly foreseen for myself. The quest for what lies beneath identity and identity politics, became my academic (and now my professional) battlefield. Perhaps I would go so far as to label it my own jihad. The richness of the traditions that form my background; the heterogeneities of this monolith that has been created and persists in the popular imagination; shattering the myth of the 'clash of civilizations' – these have become my life's work.

My crisis of faith and my crisis of identity have become enmeshed despite my best efforts to keep them separate. Perhaps, this is an opportunity to make a change for the better as one of my mentors said to me. Or perhaps I choose to see an opportunity in this and embrace it as such. Ever since leaving London more than a year ago, I have visited several countries with large young Muslim populations. India, Indonesia, Malaysia have all provided me with the opportunities to meet with people – young Muslims – who have had experiences like mine or experiences other than mine. But in every case they have had to confront their Muslim identities in one way or another. There are lessons to be learnt from each and every one of those individuals. There are voices waiting to be heard and they cannot afford to keep silent any longer. As debates become more confrontational and the 'clash of civilizations' becomes closer to a self-fulfilling prophecy, it is imperative that the rich heterogeneities of the Muslim experience become as much a part of the popular imagination as the increasingly vociferous debates on everything from the burka to the minarets to the Sharia.

Increasingly I have begun to feel that perhaps the victims of the terrorists are not simply the many that they have maimed and killed (and continue to do so). Muslim populations the world over have become the biggest victims of their tactics. Islam today feels like a religion under siege as much from within as from without. For better or worse it is up to the people of my generation to stand up and face up to the facts and begin working toward resolving this. Like it or not, it has become almost morally incumbent upon us to do so.

FLIGHT FROM PAKISTAN

AMMAR ALI QURESHI

Ammar Ali Qureshi is a London-based finance professional who has worked in areas such as investment banking, private equity, energy consulting and carbon trading. He did his Masters in Finance at Imperial College London as a Chevening Scholar. He has an MBA from Lahore University of Management Sciences (LUMS), Pakistan's most prestigious business school. He frequently contributes to different English newspapers and magazines in Pakistan such as Dawn, Daily Times and The Friday Times — mostly on subjects such as history, international relations and cultural issues.

I WAS in Islamabad, Pakistan, when 7/7 happened, but I was scheduled to move to the UK two weeks after the event. In fact I had missed the most important news during the day, as I was too busy running around trying to wrap up things, and came to know about the tragic event at dinner time when a friend told me about it at my university's alumni get-together. I was telling my friend about my scheduled move to London in about two weeks' time and he divulged the news about the events which came to be known as 7/7. I was shocked to hear the news and expressed disbelief. The news rendered me speechless for few minutes as my heart sank. To be honest, I did not take much interest in what was happening at the alumni get-together as my mind kept wondering if it is the right time to move in view of the events which happened that day.

My tension and apprehension increased further as just three days before my flight, another plot was uncovered in London, culprits were apprehended and disaster was averted. Most disturbingly, just a day before my flight, London police shot, by mistake, a Brazilian immigrant in the Underground thinking that he was a terrorist. My father, a retired senior police officer, warned me that the situation seemed to be getting really nasty and if I felt at any stage that situation is getting worse for Pakistani immigrants, I should not waste my time in London but come back immediately. I nodded my head conveying my agreement with his telling words.

Going away from your homeland is always a painful experience, especially when you are parting with your elderly parents; but there is always some enthusiasm also in moving to a new country – which in this case was not entirely new, as I had previously studied at Imperial College London and had friends and family here whom I visited regularly. However, when I boarded the plane on 23rd of July 2005, I remained very pensive and apprehensive throughout the flight hardly speaking to anyone in the plane, totally engrossed in my own thoughts. Of course the pain of separation from my parents had its telling effect on me but, undoubtedly, I was pensive about my future career in London and apprehensive about life and opportunities, given the recent ugly turn of events which had dampened my spirit and given rise to anxiety. One could not have chosen a worse time than this to migrate to the United Kingdom!

I remember my first serious conversation with my sister's family in London was about 7/7. My friends and family warned me that I should delay my job search and settle down for a couple of weeks, as it was considered prudent to avoid the Underground for about two weeks. I also realised that most of my friends preferred to speak to me on the phone instead of visiting me in Ilford, where I was staying.

Although I heeded the advice of my family and friends and delayed my job search and avoided the Underground for a couple of weeks, to let the dust settle down, I figured out that it is impossible to avoid the Underground for long as my life would come to a standstill. My conversations with my friends centred on my job prospects under changed circumstances, something I had not even imagined in my wildest dreams when I took the decision of applying for immigration to the UK. Most of the friends were cautious in their advice but all repeated the obvious; I could not have chosen a worse time to start looking for a job as a new immigrant. My exchange of views with my friends made me quite nervous and I started questioning the wisdom of my decision to move to the UK, as I had a decent job and comfortable lifestyle in Pakistan.

During the first six months of my stay, I came across a number of people from my country and the discussion, invariably, came round to 7/7 and its aftermath. All of them expressed disbelief and shock over the event and most of them felt ashamed that in this cowardly and ghastly terrorist act, most of the people involved were linked to our country of origin. Some of the people, not very educated, expressed denial as they thought Muslims could not have done this and came up with all types of conspiracy theories to shift the blame on others. However, the number of people who denied the involvement of Pakistanis was few and most of the people agreed, although they felt ashamed, that the people involved were linked to our country. Subsequent plots which were uncovered also exposed links to our country of origin and obviously after some time even those who initially denied the involvement of Pakistanis in 7/7 came to realise that there was definitely the involvement of local, young British-Pakistani men in these events. The most disturbing point was that just a handful of men had brought a bad name to the whole community, their country of origin and their religion. The whole community felt as if their identity had been hijacked by a small group of brainwashed young men with perverted ideas.

At the same time, the media coverage was quite negative and biased against Muslims. This negative portrayal and stereotyping of young Muslims put them on the defensive and further reinforced their problems of bias and discrimination against them on the street level. Young Muslims were not only on the defensive but also displayed a siege mentality, as if the media were waging a war against them and there were concerted efforts to defame them publicly. It was quite difficult to argue and convince people who were showing signs of paranoia. However, one had to keep hammering the point that we should not be displaying any illegal or unlawful behaviour as this would reinforce the negative image that is being shown by the media. My interaction with the people of the community made me aware of the problems being faced by the community as I heard stories of bias and discrimination. It made me feel very sad as there was a feeling of indignation and fear experienced by quite a few members of the community whom I met.

On a personal level, I must state that my apprehensions of discrimination against Muslims and Pakistanis turned out to be wrong. During my stay in the UK, I cannot even recall one instance of discrimination or racial abuse. No one has blamed me or my country or religion for 7/7 as far as my personal interaction with other communities is concerned. In this respect, all my apprehensions in the initial few days of my settling down in the UK turned out to be misplaced. One of the reasons can be that I belong to that class of society which has advantage of higher education in this country. Most of my social circle consists of highly educated professionals, and the work place also has a wide variety of people from different backgrounds.

I have faced quite a few problems in getting jobs due to the poor economic environment or lack of UK job experience (when I arrived in the UK in the initial years, this point was quite common when I was interviewed by different people) but no one has raised any issue about my ethnic or religious background. The only time I faced a remark about my country of origin and religion was when I was offered a job and my future boss commented in a light-hearted manner: "I know you are a Pakistani Muslim with moderate, not extreme, views." We both had a laugh and I explained it to him that most Pakistanis are Muslims with moderate views and are law-abiding citizens of this country. It is just a handful of brainwashed men who have brought infamy to the whole community and distorted their image.

I always thought that the Western media debates about Islam were biased. When it comes to Islamic dressing – the hijab or burka – their belief in their own values such as freedom of choice does not seem very robust. Although personally I am not in favour of the burka, whether in the West or the Muslim countries, I think the timing for such sensitive debates is misplaced, and could end up inflaming passions among the Muslim community who may take refuge in the most reactionary or conservative interpretation of Islam. This shift to conservatism is quite understandable when the perception among agitated young Muslims is that their lifestyle and religious values are under assault by the West and their media. I think these debates have to wait for another day to take place in a more relaxed environment.

Events such as 7/7 and 9/11 and other acts should not be seen in isolation from the Palestinian issue and other flash-points, where Muslims feel they are being deprived of their legitimate rights, and perceive the West as an imperialistic hegemony out there to impose its values. Unless some success is achieved on the foreign policy front which can be used to convince Muslims that the West is fair and even-handed in its treatment of Muslims across the world, it is better to delay discussion on sensitive religious matters such as the burka or Sharia. Any imposition of Western views on an already beleaguered Muslim community would be counterproductive and would produce an extreme reaction which can further damage the current situation instead of bringing on any improvement or progress.

The tragic event of 7/7 had an impact on my personality also, as it made me live in a quite different environment that I had imagined when taking the decision to move to the UK. Instead of becoming more defensive, I have become more open to ideas from the other side. However, I do believe in engaging the other side in polite conversation and try to express the concerns and perceptions of which they might be unaware. As I have not experienced any discrimination or bias myself, my contribution has been to convey the feelings, concerns and perceptions of those who have experienced it to those who might not be aware of the point of the view of the people being subjected to this discrimination. I think it is important to play this role, in whatever small capacity I can – as most of my opinions are restricted to my circle of friends and acquaintances.

I had not been able to do any voluntary work till now as my job required a lot of international travel, and as a result I could not dedicate much time to volunteer work on regular basis. However, my interaction with the members of my community does take place quite regularly and I always try to wean them away from conservative ideas. Most of the people I meet in my community are law-abiding peaceful citizens; they do not have extreme views but they do have conservative views on religious issues which have become intertwined with ethnic and identity issues in some cases.

I feel that the Muslim community in Britain needs successful role models to look up to. As long as the Muslim community does not produce a large number of role models who have been very successful in this society, it is but natural for the young Muslims growing up in this country to seek inspiration from abroad. There are role models produced by the Muslim and Pakistani community but they need to be projected properly by the media as well, since they have a significant role in creating models for the youth of the community. The best way to wean away young Muslims from extreme views is to reinforce their belief and sell them the idea that people from their community are doing very well in this country and it is these role models that they should be following instead of someone abroad.

It is definitely the responsibility of successful Pakistanis in the country to acknowledge their role and do their bit to engage members of their community, guide them and reinforce the belief of the members of the community in their ability and in the possibility of doing well in this society if they work hard and take advantage of opportunities being offered. In addition it is also important for civil society and political party platforms, representing Pakistanis and Muslims, to defend their community and present their case more forcefully to the authorities, and influence the media to change their tone and negative stereotyping of the Muslim community. Concerted efforts have to be made by the community platforms which belong to civil society and political organisations. Sometimes one feels that religious organisations in the UK which are linked to Pakistan and other Muslim countries are better organised and funded than political and civil society organisations. These liberal and progressive organizations need to play an important role as a counterweight to religious organizations operating in the country. These platforms need to become more active and functional so that they can compete with religious organisations in mobilising community members and wean them away from just listening to religious leaders on issues affecting their lives. As long as Muslim civil society and political organisations do not take up their role, religious organisations will continue to exert influence on the members of the community.

At a personal level, I have been affected in intellectual and spiritual terms by events such as 7/7. It has made me more reflective, more analytical and honed my desire to understand more about my religion, especially its long neglected spiritual and mystic currents. I think it is important that one draws inspiration from these well established tolerant traditions within Islam. This deserves to be highlighted as a counterweight to the intolerant strands in religion which has driven people to despair and nihilism. This inner struggle has refined me as a human being, and made me more open and tolerant towards other communities and other religions. It is a shame that the Sufi tradition of Islam is neglected by both members of the community as well as the West. The discourse in the West has unfortunately focused on the intolerant and illiberal strand within Islam and has ignored the Sufi tradition, which has always won heads and hearts in South Asia for centuries.

It has definitely been a great experience living in the UK after 7/7, in an environment which is radically different from what I had imagined it to be. I am glad that my personal apprehensions turned out to be wrong. At the same time, I have been pained to see members of my community complaining about discrimination against them in the current environment in which media coverage has resulted in a negative stereotype.

Bridging
the Divide

Seja Majeed

Seja Majeed is British Iraqi law graduate living in North London. She recently won an award by V-inspired the National Volunteer's Service, for being the most inspirational volunteer for Greater London. Seja is one of the first young Muslim women to be chosen in a national advertising campaign for V-inspired, the leading volunteer charity for young people.

7/7 is not just a number, date, or a sentiment. It is a memory shared by millions and never to be forgotten. I can remember the day exactly, a feeling of nervousness spread through me as I turned on my television only to be greeted by the shocking news. The noise of police cars and ambulances racing in the background where I lived was what had initially propelled me to switch on my TV in the first place. Something was obviously wrong in the world and my instincts proved correct. I was speechless as I heard the BBC news reporter state that four suicide explosions had been carried out in central London. I immediately knew that Pandora's Box had been opened; it would take a miracle to undo the negative repercussions that the Muslim community would experience as a result. The September 11th aftermath acted as a testimony to the potential backlash of hatred that could revive. Now ordinary Muslims like me would have to pay the price for the actions of a select few.

More than anything, it was the realisation that the whole world was watching that made my stomach sink. It was only natural for me to wonder what people around the globe were thinking about my beautiful religion, Islam. I have never been ashamed of my religious beliefs, but I was certainly ashamed of those men who pretended to act in accordance to its divine teachings. Quite clearly they knew nothing about Islam's peaceful or respectful heart. Since September 11th I had felt the need to defend Islam from those who suggest it was nothing more than a terrorist ideology. It seemed my efforts had been lost in vain just like so many others, who had to once again cement broken bridges.

What made matters worse was the visual images that haunted our TV screens. The majority of Muslims within the United Kingdom are moderates, with an overwhelming proportion of Muslims condemning the violence, and yet the British Media had invited speakers like Abu Hamza, or Captain Hook, to express what Muslims were thinking. Every time he spoke I instinctively changed the channel unable to listen to the man who preached violence as if it was something commendable.

Some people blamed the 7/7 terrorist acts on British foreign policy and the war in Iraq and Afghanistan. It was an argument that was commonly used, one which kept on creeping into the discussion forum just like a slogan that was hooked on replay. Eventually the argument started to desensitize the listener. The more I listened to the news, the more I began to realise that no one could actually explain why these British Muslims had attacked their own people. Their reasons could have been anything, from social hardship, economic instability, political frustration or psychological trauma. There was no explanation of the problem and thus, no viable solution. Passionate politics had finally come alive but for the wrong reasons. All the while I sat there, listening and thinking about tomorrow and how I would have to leave my house and somehow interact with a society that was enraged and rightly so.

On the 8th of July, I gathered the courage to leave the confines of my house and headed out into the danger zone. I remember my father telling me to be cautious; I could tell he was afraid about retaliation against Muslims. It was, after all, expected. Stories already circulated about how some Muslim women were being attacked on the streets because they wore the hijab. One woman had her headscarf ripped off in Bradford, or so my father told me. The trouble was I lived only a short distance away from Edgware Road Underground Station, the very heart of where one of the suicide attacks had taken place. I can vividly remember putting on my headscarf with a sense of dread taking hold of me. My hands became heavy like stone as I folded the material and pinned it together. I had always believed in freedom, justice and respect, and yet the intensity of wearing this symbol over my head was now foreseen as a form of persecution. I could not imagine how it felt to be a woman, who wore a burka, although I do not completely agree with the idea of covering your face, I nevertheless respect a woman's right to do so.

Walking through the streets of London was not the greatest obstacle. It was being confined in public places that felt painfully difficult. People were staring at me, looking at my scarf and glaring at my bag as if I possessed some form of ammunition that would unexpectedly explode. If they had looked into my bag they would have found a tonne of law books, with scribbled notes on freedom, justice and liberty. Either way, they did not need to say anything. I could see the immense fear that lingered in their eyes. They all possessed the same type of glare, you know the kind that was long, judgmental and absorbed one's energy from the confines of one's body. Even so, I did not blame anyone for this type of reaction; I myself had become conscious of people.

On 9th July, most Underground stations had reopened after the service had been temporarily closed. As I waited on the Victoria line platform, a human voice bellowed on the microphone speakers, "If you see anyone acting suspiciously, please report it to a member of staff." Naturally, eyes shift towards me and those who appeared to fit the description of being a 'Muslim'. In a way I wanted to prove my friendly nature by smiling at people. The gesture had worked on some, but not on everyone. The situation oddly reminded me of George Orwell's novel 1984, except the situation was no longer fictional or pleasurable to read. The worst feeling was sitting in a carriage, and watching passengers hold up newspapers with images of the aftermath spread across it. Wherever you looked you would see a line of ghastly images with anti-Islamic slogans. It made the journey much more difficult to endure, but the feeling of anger was common. I felt it also.

On 22nd July, shocking news once again resurfaced through the power of the media. This time I had heard the news on the radio when I was driving to Brunel University. The news was deeply tragic and heart wrenching. Jean Charles de Menezes, a Brazilian young man, had been shot in the head seven times at Stockwell Underground Station and killed after being wrongly suspected of being a suicide bomber. The police had now adopted a 'shoot to kill' practice, which had fatal consequences for anyone who was in the wrong place at the wrong time. An innocent death had once again been added to the long list of numbers that haunted society. It felt like the world was crumbling into pieces, and our future was no longer one that provided optimism for the next generation. I remember my mother being nervous every time my brother left the house, the idea that someone could be shot dead because they appeared Middle Eastern left her with an irrational feeling of fear. This was propelled by the fact that my mother had already lost two brothers by execution from Saddam Hussein's Ba'ath regime in Iraq. I remember trying to calm my mother every time my brother came back home late. Naturally she feared the worst.

Days, weeks and years have passed since the horrific suicide attacks took place on 7th July 2005. And yet to me, it feels like it only happened yesterday; the memories are still vivid and the feelings are as painful to endure. The world has not progressed very much since then; after all terrorist attacks commonly make their way into our newspapers, TV screens and radio broadcasts. The only distinction is that they have not surfaced here within my home country, but I would not hold my breath on that. The world remains in a state of global calamity, one that is far from being resolved or even likely to be resolved. Nothing I can say can undo what has happened; it is now a part of our modern history that will be dwelt upon for many years to come. Every era will be defined with one experience that is likely to overshadow all others and I believe that the 21st century will always be overshadowed by the rise of the fanatical extremism of a select few.

I have always believed that humanity's past actions have the capacity to haunt our future. It is now up to us to correct the negative repercussions that have emerged as a consequence of ignorance. Since 7/7 I have devoted myself entirely in trying to build bridges where they have been torn apart. The process has been extremely hard and the battle has been more than intense, but the cause has always been worth the struggle. Throughout this experience I have never felt vulnerable or afraid of what others may think; instead I have only felt bitter sadness for what has happened. The 7/7 terrorist attack was one that was directed at every person who stands for the sanctity of life and the ideology of freedom, justice and liberty. The enemy is not Islam or Muslims, it is the individual who refuses to respect the sanctity of human life and so takes his frustrations out on society by horrific means. A divide has emerged between people caused by anger and fuelled by ignorance. It is precisely this gap that I have tried to work on.

In 2007, I journeyed to my homeland Iraq, a place destroyed by war and torn apart by frequent terrorist attacks. I had gone there to deliver humanitarian supplies. It was painful to see Iraq in such a state, but my experience did not leave me with bitterness recoiling in my mouth; quite the contrary. It made me look forward to the future, because I believe that this era has reached the lowest point imaginable, and therefore, it can only get better if we focus our full attention on improving it. So long as we begin to rebuild ourselves, replace ignorance with knowledge and work collectively to overcome these obstacles, we can have a prosperous future for the next generation. The one thing that has left me with bitter anger is the advantage gained by fascist parties such as the British National Party and radical clerics, who have exploited people's fear and used it to cultivate a following. Since the 7/7 bombings a new rise in extremism has emerged from both spectrums, it is this that is adding fuel to the fire. A new crusade or jihadist movement is expanding, and if we are not vigilant and careful, we will all be victims of their propaganda and war.

They say time is a great healer but, like many people, I cannot forget where I was or how I felt on the day of 7/7. Neither can I forget how much more difficult life became thereafter. It feels almost dreamlike to even speculate. Would it have been easier for me as a Muslim woman to have got a job if it were not for 7/7? Would I still experience the upsetting phrase of being called a 'terrorist' or 'fanatic' because I wear the headscarf? These are just some of the questions that revolve in my mind and slowly eat away at my thoughts. But I do not consider myself as a victim of the aftermath of 7/7; rather I am inspired to bring about a change. After all, our actions must be drawn proudly in dedication to all the innocent victims around the world who have suffered at the hands of global terrorism. This is the least that we can do in remembrance of their names.

So I stand firm and am proud to say that I am a British Iraqi Muslim woman and there will be nothing that can make me draw back in shame or retreat from this ongoing battle. 7/7 may testify to the destruction and hurt that a few individuals can cause in our society. But for me it acts as a reminder of my purpose, which is to unite people, protect freedom and shield our society from further calamities.

FROM TYRANNY TO TERROR

HASSAN ALKATIB

Born to Iraqi parents, Hassan moved to London at the age of three. At 17, he went on to study Media at West Herts College. Many of his works include a documentary about his trip to Iraq during Christmas 2005, and a short, creative video which was screened at the Young Co-operative Film Festival in Yorkshire, 2006. He made his documentary 'The British Muslim Struggle' in his spare time during the final two years of his course at university. Hassan now works as a video editor and documentary filmmaker at Press TV.

ON the morning of the 7th of July, I vividly remember turning on the television and seeing the images of the number 30 bus with the roof blown off. I instantly knew this was serious and dreaded the anti-Muslim backlash that would take place. My sister had been using the London Underground in the city centre when the bombings happened. Thankfully, she was unharmed. My relatives in Iraq phoned us to know whether we were affected. I felt quite ashamed knowing that, living in London, I am virtually free of any threat of being bombed, whereas in some parts of Iraq – especially the capital – such threats are a daily occurrence. However, my family and I have always contacted our relatives in Iraq when a bombing happens near their area – as family ties are very important in Islam.

Information of the attack gradually developed and the official narrative pointed to four male suicide-bombers from Yorkshire. I was not prepared to believe anything unless there was good, hard evidence. It did not take a genius to work out that the bombers did this because they were angry about Britain's support for Israel and occupation in Iraq and Afghanistan. The video of Mohammad Sidique Khan, aired on Al-Jazeera shortly after 7/7, was further confirmation that the attacks were politically motivated. The government was in denial about this and tried to pretend the bombers' faith was the underlying factor.

I live in a very multi-racial and multicultural area in London. Instances of Islamophobic attacks are rare, so I never really felt the threat of being physically or verbally attacked. The then Mayor of London, Ken Livingstone gave a strong speech in Trafalgar Square, in which he made it clear that Londoners must not be divided. But with all the good words, there still was a heightened climate of fear and prejudice which resulted in attacks against Muslims. The Mosque I regularly prayed in had some of its windows smashed, and graffiti had been sprayed on a bus stop with the words: Bomb the Muslims. Not to mention the dead hedgehogs thrown at the front of our house on the anniversary of 9/11.

A few months after the 7/7 bombings, I was stopped by a middle-aged man as I was on my way back from college. He asked me if I had a gun in my bag. I replied "No I don't"; he then asked me if I was carrying a bomb. I said "No" again, at which point he looked over his shoulder to a couple of men standing close by, and said to them "It's alright". That was probably the first time I had been stereotyped in such a manner. In some ways I actually consider myself lucky that it did not turn out worse. Nevertheless, I tried not to take it too personally and put it behind me. Part of this witch-hunt against British Muslims emanated from certain sections of the mainstream media, particularly the right-wing press.

Many Islamophobic commentators used 7/7 to spout hatred and instil fear among readers and viewers to further their agenda. I strongly feel that some of this demonisation was done deliberately and not out of ignorance. 7/7 also unleashed a torrent of discourses. I read articles questioning whether multiculturalism was acceptable, to the so-called 'problem' of Islam itself. British Muslims were quizzed about their loyalty to the nation, and were often portrayed as 'fifth columnists'. I started to watch and analyse a lot of documentaries about Muslims broadcast on terrestrial television. I became conscious of how some of the programmes distorted and misrepresented Islam. I knew the negative impact this would have if such programming went unchallenged. Thanks partly to the 'open season' against Muslims in the media – many reports revealed the huge rise in Islamophobic attacks across the country.

As a media student at the time, 7/7 gave me a nudge, but was not the sole factor in shaping my aims for the future. I had always felt it to be my religious, civic and moral duty to counter some of the lies, ignorance and misinformation about Islam and Muslims, as I believed this would stem the flow of hatred, discrimination and violent attacks, and foster better ties among different cultures and communities, more so after 7/7.

At college I produced a 12-minute documentary about the misconceptions regarding Islam. The aim was to raise awareness of the Islamic faith and build bridges between Muslims and non-Muslims. It argued how some terrorist attacks, for instance, have been carried out by people under the name of Christianity, yet we seem to think only Muslims are terrorists. It also highlighted how fringe extremists like Omar Bakri, Abu Hamza and Osama Bin Laden do not represent Islam and Muslims, and in actual fact have misunderstood their own religion. The programme included short interviews with members of the public, who were asked six simple yes-no questions about Islam – some of which were: "Do Muslims believe in Jesus and Mary?"; "Is Islam tolerant of other faiths?" And "Does Jihad mean Holy War?" Results showed a mixture of correct and incorrect answers with a significant number saying 'don't know'. My documentary was well received, by colleagues and teachers alike. Most were in shock to learn about these misconceptions, and at one point a friend of mine confessed he was absolutely unaware that misunderstandings of Islam even existed!

As a British Muslim growing up in the current climate, I have been very much politicised. However, I would not say 7/7 was a pivotal point in my lifetime nor, so much, 9/11. It was mainly my parents and their families' forced exile from Iraq in the early 1980s that served as a springboard of political savviness. They were exiled because they stood up against Saddam Hussein's dictatorship. Three of my uncles were imprisoned and later executed for their opposition against the regime. So from an early age I was always taught to stand up against injustices, wherever they may be. That is why I have always maintained a strong stance against the war in Iraq. I knew the US-led invasion in 2003 was wrong, as it embodied an imperial agenda that sought to divide and dominate the region. There were mixed reactions amongst British Iraqis on whether the war should go ahead. True, Saddam was a brutal ruler and he oppressed and killed his people, but it was the CIA who put him in power and supported him in the first place. I was overjoyed to see millions of people in London protesting against the war in Iraq. My Iraqi identity did not make me in any way vulnerable; on the contrary, many people were sympathetic towards me upon knowing where I was originally from.

Most British Muslims I have met, including many British Iraqis, are concerned about our country's domestic and foreign policy. They feel the British government has not helped, but rather hindered community relations in response to 7/7. Tough 'anti-terror' laws were introduced that unfairly targeted British Muslims. The 'Prevent' agenda promoted Muslim groups and individuals who would not criticise them over foreign policy. MI5 used intimidatory and harassing techniques against Muslims. Testimonies found that our government was complicit in torturing Muslims abroad. This and the continuing support for Israel and dictatorships in the Muslim world, have all contributed to alienating and demonising British Muslims. The government has been fuelling extremism, not preventing it. With so many other obstacles, compounded with Islamophobia and the current plight of the Muslim world, it is no wonder that a defeatist attitude has crept in – further isolating and disenfranchising British Muslims from the political system and mainstream society. I believe the need to engage and become active at the local, national and international level is an important stepping-stone to address the grievances and issues of the day. So this is where my work, as a film documentary maker, can play a positive role, whereby I encourage and empower Muslims and non-Muslims for the betterment of society and the world. I only wish more and more academic, intelligent and representative British Muslims would enter the media, especially the mainstream. That way it would allow British Muslims to speak for themselves as well as take proactive measures in helping to break down barriers as opposed to merely reacting when the damage is already done.

My best work to date is a self-funded documentary entitled: 'The British Muslim Struggle'. Half-an-hour long, the programme provides an insight into the role of British Muslim activists and lobbyists, highlighting the importance of civic engagement and political participation. It addresses some of the major obstacles British Muslims face and attempts to show how they can overcome these hurdles.

I sent copies of my documentary to prominent Muslim organisations and individuals asking them to write a short review in order to promote my work. I received a lot of praise and I would not be writing this essay if Murtaza Shibli had not seen my film. I later went on to sell the programme to Press TV, an international news and current affairs channel. I was then employed at the channel as recognition for my filmmaking and video editing skills. The documentary has since been broadcast and is available online.

This work is a great example of what one person can do. I have gained so much experience and knowledge in my field and it was all down to a desire to make a change. If I had any advice to the youth of today, I would tell them not to waste their time. To make good use of the opportunities that are there in front of them. To believe in what you do and most importantly, as the saying goes, 'Do your best, and God will do the rest'.

Because of this documentary, I have learnt a lot about the topic I covered. I was completely unaware of how the UK political system worked. Lobbying did not just consist of writing letters and holding demonstrations, it involved a whole system of public relations. I never really knew much about the House of Commons, or how laws are made. I felt really uneducated about a subject matter that is of utmost importance to the health of our democracy. Understanding the political system paves the way for more, productive engagement, and the responsibility lies with us, as well as the government, public institutions, Islamic centres, Mosques etc. to help inform citizens of their rights and duties.

I am at ease with my religious and national identity. I feel British because I have come to learn more about this country's history, its laws, democracy and freedoms, most of which go hand in hand with Islam. Islam itself has been a great source of inspiration throughout my life and because of that I have a clear vision and purpose, without which I would not have found it possible to realise my potential.

REFLECTIONS
OF A STUDENT

NADA MANSY

Nada Mansy is British-Egyptian and a recent graduate of the London School of Economics and Political Science (LSE) where she read Sociology. Born in the ancient coastal town of Alexandria in Egypt, she moved to the UK at the age of seven with her parents and elder sister. Her father's occupation in the NHS led to a peripatetic upbringing with homes across the South of England before her family settled in East Sussex. Alongside her studies Nada became engaged in local youth-politics. She later further immersed herself in this during her undergraduate studies at the LSE. There she received an award for her student activism and her work in the LSE Students Union Islamic Society (ISoc). Nada currently works in a voluntary capacity for the Federation of Student Islamic Societies (FOSIS) and has a long term interest in teaching and community work.

IT was a warm summer day of 2005. That late afternoon I strolled into the living room and switched on the television. But what I saw made no sense. Why were there so many policemen on the screen? Where did all the debris come from? Why were people crying? We see these gut wrenching scenes of pain and distress daily on our television screens. But this was London, this was home.

As the unsightly, raw truth came to light, it took on an identity of its own. 7/7 has none of the cold, impersonal, factual sensations of a historical event. Remembering what happened even now brings with it that hot, sickening feeling that horror films seek to market clashing with the hurtful sentiment of those that say "we've heard it all before, yes, yes, it's very sad". I wonder if those voices would echo the same words had it been their loved ones on the tube that morning. Every tear, every drop of blood is precious, wherever it is in the world, whenever the time, whatever the circumstances. As often quoted,

"... if anyone slays a human being ... — it shall be as though he had slain all mankind; whereas, if anyone saves a life, it shall be as though he had saved the lives of all mankind..."

Quran 5:32

147

If only the world lived up to this universal guidance.

In the ensuing media coverage of 7/7 I heard news report after news report and journalist after journalist repeat the mantra that these attacks were perpetrated by 'Muslim terrorists' in the name of Islam. I was numb. I sank. I was resolute. Islam? Islam is my life. Can you imagine seeing the one thing you love more than anything be so wrongly portrayed and associated with the worst and most twisted of transgressions? Then maybe you can begin to understand how I and hundreds of millions of Muslims felt. Islam was being hijacked once more.

In the days and weeks that followed, going out as a brown-skinned hijabi in my small home-counties town was not exactly devoid of unease which I had also experienced in the aftermath of 9/11. Except this time it was different – this time, it had happened on British soil. I wondered if people would act differently. And I wondered, what's the worst that could happen; horrible remarks, abuse? But rationally, that seemed surreal. What about my old friends? Two months were left until I would start my second year of the sixth form, would they behave differently?

Even to this day, when I walk on a station platform or sit on a train, I hear "Please report any suspicious items or behaviour" and wonder if people take notice of such announcements. Do they hurriedly glance at the Muslim-looking individuals? Do they change carriages for a different seat away from me?

Perhaps I was being cynical. I do remember smiling at the old white man reading the Daily Mail near the Post Office. I was pleasantly surprised when he smiled back. And I remember taking my bag off the extra seat as a passenger came onto the crowded train. She was a wealthy professional woman, wearing designer sunglasses and carrying a leather handbag. She told me she was visiting her son, and it was nice to share a friendly conversation until she arrived at her destination. Friends of mine may be surprised to know my thoughts and feelings. But confidence, even if apparent, cannot be absolute or unwavering. I appreciate any act of kindness, however small, because I'm thankful that those people's good conduct to me hasn't been negatively influenced by the media.

My own recollection and experience, in one way, is not really that important at all because, whether or not I have felt the brunt of the change, 7/7 did change things. A new climate of suspicion and of sudden vulnerability seems to have permeated us all. In this respect, Muslims are no different to any other citizens. It seems, however, as though Muslims have come to be viewed by some as the 'other' whether or not the label is explicit. And for some Muslims, it may be easier to assume the victim mentality, to feel disempowered, to want to give up and keep their heads under the radar. That would be easy. But to think deeply and act wisely; that is the challenge that meets us all daily.

ADVENTURE AND GROUNDING

It was a clear spring day. I opened a sealed envelope to find a letter with a crested logo shining in the top right hand corner. "Dear Ms Mansy" I eagerly read line by line, none of it mattered except for one sentence I was hoping for with daydreams and high expectations tightly intertwined. I was hurriedly searching for it, and there it was. I had been offered a place to study at the prestigious London School of Economics (LSE)! I was going to university! I could not contain my excitement. And little did I know what was in store for me for the next three years; little did I know that my university experience would be far from dusty library shelves.

October 2006, a typically cold and rainy day. I opened the door, took off my shoes and felt the thick pile of carpet under my feet. I looked around; it was a small room, enclosed with warm beige walls, decorated with hand crafted oil paintings of Arabic calligraphy. On one side I saw the shelves lined with books; the Qur'ans majestically placed at the top. On the other side lay a pile of inviting Moroccan cushions. The first time I walked into the Islamic Society (ISoc) prayer room I received the warmest welcome, bright cheery faces and genuine interest, the seeds planted that evening were to nourish my entire university experience, the relationships formed would enrich my very soul and intellect.

LSE life was almost like a continuous whirlwind of activity. Between the academic lectures and classes, there was the ISoc charity fundraising one day and voting in a brimmed lecture theatre the next. From chairing a meeting then running to the debate society workshop and squeezing lunch with friends in between, it was a wonder how any of us managed to get our essays done! And throughout my time, ISoc was a constant.

What I loved most was the attitude and mindset the ISoc nurtured within us. To put it simply, the message was "Be Good People". It was to positively engage with the community around us at university, to be open and to extend the hand of friendship to all. It was to be successful in our studies, in our relationships, in our planning of the future. It was to have good intentions behind everything we do, and to always remember the higher purpose in our lives.

Here and now having left LSE with these warm memories from the ISoc, it was with utter shock to learn the alleged perpetrator of the Christmas 2009 bomb-plot was a former ISoc President, and it was a further shock to see that some parts of the media started accusing ISocs of being hotbeds of extremism. Once again that sinking feeling washed over me. Right, so it would seem that an alleged would-be terrorist once belonged to an ISoc; ergo we're all potential terrorists now?

As it happened, LSE was just across the road from University College London (UCL) where the alleged terrorist used to study. And their Vice Chancellor Malcolm Grant was reassuringly quick off the mark with his refreshing and astute comments. "Here is a sensible voice" we thought, as we breathed out a collective sigh of relief. Because there is no credible evidence to suggest British campuses are hotbeds of violent extremist thought. In fact research shows Muslim students are more likely to join Amnesty International (AI). Not quite Al-Qaida (AQ). So sorry folks, the AIs are winning over the AQs.

I know so many Muslim students who will attest to the fact that it is through an ISoc that Muslim students find a safe space to explore and ground themselves in their religious identity, a grounding which helps them lead an upright, positive life. It is ISocs that build within Muslim students a civic conscience and it is ISocs that make a tremendous contribution to university life and wider society. Is it not clear that government, universities and society at large have a responsibility to support and uphold the work of Muslim students and ISocs in these trying times?

STRENGTH IN DIVERSITY

A little while after graduating I went on a two-week leadership programme, an initiative between the Prince's Trust and Oxford University. I was part of diverse group of young Muslims, meeting an equally diverse group of speakers, from the

BBC journalist to the financial expert. On one day as we listened to the seasoned diplomat talk of his opinions on freedom of speech, the youth worker from Bradford put him on the spot. I looked at the accountant to my right (who, by the way, is a rapper by night); and he gave me a knowing look. Every day we entered the grand hall, its mahogany walls lined with portraits of those who sat at the very tables we were now at, gazing down upon us. Immaculately presented meals were set down in front of us, and each was engaged in deep conversation, the southern prison chaplain with the northern police woman, the medic (and joker of the group) with the aspiring lawyers. Looking around, I could see the potential and the success of the Muslim community just from the presence of the people in the room. And to think Prince Charles called a reunion a few months later and that we even got to have lunch at Buckingham Palace! Who would've thought this would happen a few decades ago?

As we all left energised and confident, my path took me to the Federation of Student Islamic Societies (FOSIS), where I started working with some incredible Muslims. These were young dynamic people balancing their careers or juggling their studies with their passion for community work. Day in and day out, they strove to educate people on campus and strengthen ISocs. I was awestruck, and witnessing the plethora of work FOSIS do, I only felt lucky to be a part of that.

One memorable time I recall are the weeks that followed the alleged Christmas bomb plot. It was easy to sense the frustration with ISocs unfairly cast under the spotlight, FOSIS was bent over backwards, working 24/7 liaising with ISocs, the National Union of Students, the government and media at large to make sure the true message got across. In the blizzard of meetings and discussions, the best email I received was one of the shortest – it had no words, but just a small picture attached, and we did exactly what it said;

Because we had to.

I soon found myself on a plane flying to Cologne as a UK delegate for a European-wide strategic management course. I met student activists from the small suburbs of Sweden to the urban hubs of Italy, and it struck me that we shared the same values and principles but they faced bigger challenges. It was a timely reminder that although sometimes tough, UK Muslims in some respects have it better than other European Muslims, who often face more outright, frequent and public Islamophobia. One young French Tunisian from Vaulx-en-Velin was recounting to me her parents' anxieties over the racist remarks received by the French women who choose to wear the hijab. In speaking to her further, it seemed her relationship with the state was far less developed than mine. At least many UK Muslims feel confident enough to demonstrate, to write to their MPs and to join advocacy groups.

REALITY CHECK

Yet, coming home and taking a cursory look at the headlines, optimism flirts with naivety. I switch on the television to hear about the violent stabbing of Marwa El Sherbini, the law-abiding Muslim woman in Germany, and imagine her three year old son watch his own mother slump to the floor. I read the newspaper to find the story of the London gang stabbing of three Muslim students. I log onto my email to find an article about an arson attack against a London mosque. And every time, I wonder what makes it acceptable to harm other human beings for no good reason? Which community has ever done anything to deserve pariah status? At first glance they seem to be isolated incidents, unfortunate but unusual. But sadly, in paying attention it seems to me they are too frequent, too widespread geographically. Perhaps the pattern is becoming too clear; Islamophobia is on the rise. Is this the legacy of 7/7? Living in fear and mistrust? In hate?

It seems that Islamophobia or anti-Muslim bigotry is sometimes incorrectly explained away by the potential terrorist threat post-7/7. Yet academic studies have published report upon report pointing to the same facts. I mean, I was surprised to read in one report that most UK terrorist incidents happen in Northern Ireland, relating to the troubles. It seems as though Islam is not the only religion being hijacked for political ends! And across the wider landscape in Europe, 99% of terrorist attacks were carried out by non-Muslims, not really something we hear about. And what about the UK Security Services who state terrorists are: "a diverse collection of individuals, fitting no single demographic profile, nor do they all follow a typical pathway to violent extremism." Further "most are religious novices, do not practice their faith regularly and lack religious literacy."

Surely, this is at odds with some existing views on UK national security? And having read this, the importance of ISocs was made even clearer to me.

So why does it feel like in tackling these important issues, the public instead become spectators to political football? It appears that too often the distinction between violent and non-violent groups has been blurred by some politicians and parts of the media. Along with this, Islamism and political Islam are terms habitually used with ignorance of their actual meaning and demonised as a threat. I worry when young Muslims around me listen to some politicians' well-intentioned efforts to appeal to the Muslim community, but hear the message to only get involved enough to tick political boxes – not enough to actually influence anything. For them, campaigning against western foreign policy carries with it extra baggage, more than the banner carried by the white liberal marching next to them. Such profiling arouses in them the feeling that Muslims and Islam are seen through the prism of security. Why does it seem like we are in a vicious cycle?

If so, we're doing ourselves a disservice, because to have different rules for Muslims, to not confront Islamophobia and sideline British Muslims from real political engagement will only endanger us all. When a western liberal society functions on fear and rejection of 'the other' it risks losing the very values and fundamental principles it fought for, the freedom, liberty and democracy it cherishes. I fear we're making it easier than it should be for those in the far right drawn to violence towards Muslims. I also fear we're fuelling the hatred of the minority drawn towards indiscriminate violence in response to British foreign policy.

A solution? We need greater education and cross cultural understanding. We need to gain the trust of all communities who play a vital role in our defence from would-be terrorists. We need to allow ourselves to ascertain facts about any alleged case before jumping to conclusions. We need to uphold freedom of speech more than any other time before and get away from the hypocrisy. If the 'war on terror' is a topic that can be discussed by national newspaper columnists, why shouldn't

ISocs be able to debate it? If faith schools are an issue to be discussed, let's talk about all faith schools and not just focus on Muslim schools. If we want to discuss headscarves and veils, let's listen to what Muslim women themselves have to say.

Why should the public policy discourse solely be informed by an agenda of misunderstanding and misinformation? Surely the simplistic solutions to all the problems of the day by using immigrants as a scapegoat are to be ignored? The government just needs to be a good government! And the public needs to feel that politicians can and will draw up policies beyond the narrow lens of preparing for elections.

PERSPECTIVE AND COMPASSION

I wonder why, within my own community, there doesn't seem to be more introspection. Look at the contemporary picture; surveillance, discrimination, hate crimes. These are just some of the challenges Muslims face today, especially in the post 9/11 era. And now look back at the historic picture: beatings, humiliation and torture. These were just some of the challenges the Muslims of Mecca faced in the seventh century after embracing Islam in a polytheistic era. In perspective, what do we face today that is so different from what our forebearers faced?

In times of peace and conflict, in time of hardship and ease, in times of plenty and little; the message, the purpose, the goal is always the same. We are no different from others — we too must remember our principles. We must go on serving God through serving humanity. The worst thing for Muslims is to complain and feel the whole world is against them. To be so consumed in self-pity and to readily adopt a 'victim mentality' is not just passive, but is against the very essence of what Islam advocates. Wasn't it once said, better to light a candle than to curse the darkness?

I wonder how many candles have been lit, and how many need to be as parts of the media continue to serve a diet of frightening stories every day. I put myself in the viewers shoes and think, what if it was me? Perhaps this way we can all begin to understand why some react with the base emotions of anger and hate, and not with the confident and measured wisdom of their intelligence.

And once again I remember the people in my life whose approach has been epitomised by the latter. My memory takes me to my GCSE Religious Studies teacher, a Reverend who is one of the kindest and gentlest of people I have ever met. He explained Christianity and Islam in such a way that we were encouraged to explore, question and understand. He was someone who spurred my curiosity and made me come to love Islam. In one lesson, we all sat attentively as he explained the concept in Islam of loving for another person what we love for ourselves, a famous principle I heard over the years from the halls of a mosque to the lecture theatre of an ISoc event. So surely, no matter how ignorant someone is, out of principle we cannot lose hope in them. Remember Umar, a man at the time of the Prophet Muhammad (peace be upon him) who was known to be extremely harsh, would beat female slaves who'd become Muslim and who was the greatest enemy of Islam. Yet this man converted to Islam and became the Prophet's closest companion and one of the ten promised paradise. When immersed in the beauty of Islam, surely it is selfish not to share the universal good it advocates. A smile, a prayer, a gift. A kind word, a helping hand, a coffee.

JUST ONE IN A MILLION

So many words written after one date – one date that holds so much significance. My hope is that someone reading this may think in a new way about the reality of British Muslims. The fact is that terrorists have tried to hijack Islam. It has been misrepresented and misinterpreted. This is but just another addition to the spectrum of Muslim voices that are fighting hard to restate Islam as we see it. We're taking back Islam.

An Act of
Humiliation

Farhat Amin

Farhat Amin has a wide range of skills in project management, facilitation and networking within the voluntary sector. As a Youth Development Worker he is currently delivering a mentoring project specifically for young Muslims in order to enhance the skills of a community that is continually striving for recognition. He also enjoys performing poetry and is always looking for new ways to entertain audiences in different settings.

T HE atrocities of July 7th 2005 are still fresh in the psyche of British consciousness. These attacks were indiscriminate, impacting upon individuals and communities made up from different religions, ethnicities and cultures. And what is the reason individuals still have to remind people that we do not agree with such actions?

On the day itself London was at a standstill, it was not planned in a far away land like Baghdad or Karachi or Kabul but here in England. And this is the lesson of the July 7 bombings; that young educated men who were raised in England can actually kill innocent people. This puts the question of religion and violence at the forefront – the Qur'an is supposed to be a violent book? Does the media ever put anything positive forward? Not one thing is mentioned about the equality of women, the honouring of parents and the struggle for justice. Of course not, as violence sells papers, makes headlines and ensures that a common enemy is established.

But July 7th 2005 in all seriousness was a very upsetting and tragic moment for the history of London. Looking on at the events from the TV screens I was grateful that I was not at the scenes. I originally was supposed to be somewhere in central London – but by the grace of God I did not hear anything from the organisers. My initial reaction was being thankful but then quickly turning to sorrow that so many people were potentially killed or injured in such a disastrous incident. As the news broke I did not think with any assumptions or prejudices. I felt as a human being very saddened and started questioning the reason behind these attacks. These attacks were detested then and hated now. I am, of course, a Muslim first, but my reactions were not related to my faith – my reactions were of disgust as a person living in London. As a Muslim, I felt humiliated and utterly angered that those who claim to be religious were doing these acts in the name of God. It is quite ridiculous to call these individuals Muslims. Quite frankly they are terrorists and criminals who hijacked something for the purpose of creating panic and a mass exodus.

Not only was there a profound impact upon Londoners but there was a backlash of Islamophobia. Not only did it seem that apologetics came to the front of the discussion; we continually still have to remind others that Islam does not condone violence against innocent victims.

The media have always spun stories for their own interests and not the public interest; why should they? The media are owned by private stakeholders and to brush the whole system with one stroke may be unfair. In the majority of cases there was a heightened sense of negative attention focusing on Muslim communities. This was not helped by the fact that the Government agenda Preventing Violent Extremism (Prevent), launched in 2007, concentrates only on Muslim communities under the guise of security. Learning from the past, it is important to move away from Prevent and look more at engaging communities through empowerment and provision.

Once Prevent becomes less of a priority, the work still needs to continue. Money, resources, time and people power are still needed to ensure that Britain's Muslims are at the forefront of public discourse by leading its debates, science, engineering and academia. We were once a great nation remembered for our contributions to civilization but now we must face new challenges and again lead the way society thinks. But Prevent is not the concern of this narrative, although a large issue but of greater concern is that July 7 triggered unprecedented discrimination against one community; largely law abiding and peaceful. It is not Muslims who are problematic; it is the way some choose to show their frustrations.

This brings me to my personal story; many things have shaped my own opinions and values. The incident of 7/7 has made me much more strong-willed and confident that it is not religion that divides people but the people who hijack its shrine to bring destruction to those struggling to contribute to their communities. But myths are there to be broken. We do not label a thief with a race because it is irrelevant to the crime, we do not label a fraudster with ethnicity because it is irrelevant and we do not ask whether a murderer killed someone due to their nationality.

My question is why do we as a people give these criminals the satisfaction they seek? Islam and religion per se does not give any ounce of justification to the attacks that took place in New York, London, Glasgow or Mumbai. So why do we call these people Muslims, when in fact they have no reason to kill innocent women and children. My real reason for this piece is not only to say how, as an individual, I feel about the atrocities of 7/7, but to ask why it occurred and what lessons we can learn. We can of course look back and say it should have not happened as surely the intelligence was there. But it has happened, and what we learn is much more important.

These attacks brought disgrace to London's population and its security service. As a person I feel saddened, as a Muslim I feel ashamed but not for the reasons that the media puts out there. I do not feel that I need or should apologise for the actions of others. Blame is easy, fingers are pointed but issues need to be dealt with head on. So in some respects, although there was a negative backlash against Muslim communities, this only strengthens my own resolve and determination to work positively in a society where justice for all is of paramount importance. Rather than feeling worried or scared, I became more aware and more confident of my religion in the years that followed.

So, rather than shying away from certain things, I became more confident that Islam does not preach hatred; on the contrary, the Qur'an speaks of justice and equality. In the biography of Muhammed (peace be upon him) there are so many occasions where our Prophet lived with others peacefully, regardless of their faith, and actually migrated to Medina to escape violence. Violence should never be initiated, the only reason Muhammed (peace be upon him) went to war was to protect his people in an act of self defence. These factors continually help shape my thinking as a young person interested in dispelling myths and ensuring role models become much more visible for others to learn from. For example the good work which is carried out in communities does not receive any space in a local newspaper; it is because our contributions are only seen in terms of security. So by changing myths and by delivering projects which impact upon people in a positive way, I aim to ensure that a community empowers itself through the leadership and credibility of its own actions.

This is the reason I am involved in community initiatives, this is the reason I enjoy public speaking, this is the reason why I am delivering a mentoring project and most importantly, this is the reason I work with people. So it is not about me gaining something out of the work I do, it is about having an impact on someone else by interacting with others on a daily basis. It is not my external appearance that dispels myths, but having a conversation with someone. This can be taken to a much broader level, in that Muslims need to integrate to some extent with regard to working and socialising with others, but not to the extent that their own religious values get evaporated. Of course, Muslims want to ensure that old bridges are maintained and that new bridges are built between different communities.

The question is, has 7/7 changed the way we as individuals think, the way we interact with others, or the way we work? As a people, 7/7 exposed the fact that any city in any country is penetrable, but this has to be prevented in the future. The point of this argument is that any terrorist act of violence should be hated and, if possible, stopped. Violence cannot be applauded, and should not be celebrated by anyone regardless of the context. To claim that terrorism is an act of religion is far from the truth.

The issue of citizenship and religion is at the heart of the debate concerning terrorism. As a Muslim, my religion is of paramount importance but this does not undermine my citizenship. It is my faith that makes my contribution to society greater. For example, I believe that as a Muslim I should do my utmost to help others. And citizenship and faith are two different concepts which are part of someone's personality and self-discovery.

This sums up the argument nicely, that in order to change something, it has to be done from within. The Qur'an clearly states that whoever wishes to change will do so through personal struggle. This individual desire to change oneself needs to be shared with others, that this religion is one of empowering oneself by submitting one's will to something much greater than ourselves. This empowerment comes from the expression of faith that we do not rely on anything except God for our needs, wants and desires. This factor makes social justice prevail. If we want to be beacons of hope to others, we must be beacons of hope to ourselves. And this can only be achieved by ensuring that we become proactive and not reactive.

So what were the lessons from 7/7 and how can we take these lessons and move forward? The lessons were that we need to stop apologising for the actions of others and that we cannot box ourselves into isolation. We need to dispel myths and ensure that we are not viewed through the prism of security. And these lessons need to be put in place by all of us from the individual to the community by taking part in community projects, organising our own projects and helping others.

Although 7/7 was a disastrous day and should be remembered, we have to move on and really ask the question whether Muslims are being treated fairly, or are we as a people doing ourselves any favours. These questions have already been asked and will continually be asked but the point is how we actively pass on the message that British Muslims can offer practicability, vigour and optimism to many of the problems society is facing.

We pass on this message that we will continue to strive for justice and equality not only through words but our actions. Writing is maybe something academics do, but it is more important to utilise words and actually take these words and implement them. I first must change myself and ensure that I take a lead and help others to develop themselves and ultimately become champions of their communities.

Communities need leaders, but what good is a leader if their people are not being paid attention to? People must take responsibility for their own actions and put in place the understanding and the solutions to allow them to take control of their own lives without others dictating their decisions.

Summer of Sirens & Sleeplessness

Saadeya Shamsuddin

Saadeya Shamsuddin is a journalist, broadcaster and writer. She read the Ancient World at University College London and later gained an MA in Journalism from City University London on a scholarship awarded by the National Union of Journalists' George Viner Memorial Fund. Her postgraduate dissertation examined the portrayal of Muslim women in the British media with an accompanying series of modern portraits documenting their experiences. Saadeya trained in both print and broadcast and has worked for the Kensington & Chelsea News, the Financial Times, Sunday Times, London Evening Standard and BBC London. She was recipient of the Royal Shakespeare Company's Arts Journalist Bursary Scheme in 2009/10 and is a member of the UK Governments' Young Muslims Advisory Group (YMAG).

"The tragedy of life and of the world is not that men do not know God; the tragedy is that, knowing Him, they still insist on going their own way."
William Barclay, Theologian (1907-1978)

AS a student of classical civilization, it was part of my undergraduate degree to study the ancient Greek tragedies. Drawn to the way each poet dealt with the human condition, I was fascinated by the way emotions and circumstances developed and evolved throughout each character's personal drama. Then, just as my first year drew to a close, a real tangible tragedy unfolded before everyone's eyes. It was brutal and unexpected, but we are taught "such is life." It felt like I was part of two parallel worlds.

It was the end of my first year at University College London, on my Ancient World degree course. I had managed to land part-time student work with my university's Corporate Communications and Development office on Tottenham Court Road, a few minutes from Warren Street tube station. A group of us, from a range of courses and year groups had been selected to call alumni during the long, balmy summer evenings. We were tasked with engaging in a 'friendly chat' with former students, update their records and, most importantly, ask them to consider donating to one of six designated funds the university was raising money for, including scholarships.

Despite sounding monotonous, I found our task enjoyable, especially as I was assigned to call alumni from my own faculty, the department of Greek and Latin. Unsurprisingly, very few of them had gone into careers related to the field of ancient history, but worryingly quite a few were also unemployed. Knowledge of economic and cultural riches founded in antiquity clearly wasn't enough to translate to a well paid job in the modern world. Interestingly, at this point I had not considered journalism as a career, so was yet to be acquainted with job instability.

Our 'calling' job was to end during the first week of July. On that fateful Thursday I was due to go into work in the afternoon. I remember being home alone that morning and switching on BBC News 24 around 11 a.m. I was met with the scene of a double decker bus with its top blown off in Tavistock Square. This was around the corner from my university department at the end of Gordon Street in Bloomsbury. I was confused. I paid closer attention to the commentary on the news; the newsreader was speaking to an American tourist on the phone who had apparently witnessed the explosion. The tourist was describing the curious scene of carnage before me on the TV screen, and I distinctly remember that she had confused the route 30 bus for a tourist bus. So much for eye-witness accounts, but I guess for visitors they were all tourist buses of sorts.

There were further reports of other explosions on the tube that had happened hours earlier and I was dumbstruck. What the HELL was going on?! At that point in the day, the cause of the explosions was still unknown, and the severity of the situation had not sunk in. I don't think it did for anyone until the following days and weeks; it's almost like going into shock after a terrible event – the grief only hits you after a while.

That afternoon on BBC and ITV there was a rolling broadcast of the bomb sites across central London. It was surreal; almost as if I was watching a chaotic, bomb-ravaged metropolis in an action film, the piercing sound of police sirens filling the air. Only there was no hero – just countless innocent bystanders in a shocked stupor and us at home watching them on our TV sets. And then came the creeping thought of whether anyone you knew had been caught in the blast. A little later I received a text message. It was Charlotte, a close friend who lives in Bristol: "R u ok? x" I replied I was at home and safe in North-West London, and she texted back saying she was glad and was just checking to make sure. Of course, I could think of a hundred people I knew who may have been caught in the blasts, but most of my friends had gone back to their homes across the UK for the summer, or were on holiday. As it turned out, I was lucky not to have lost anyone on that day, but there were other families who were not so fortunate.

I soon received an e-mail from work letting the group know that the calling shift had been cancelled that evening. It was just as well given the Underground had completely shut down. Little did we know then that this day would be marked down in history for the deadliest terrorist attack in the UK since the Lockerbie bombing of the eighties. Another e-mail followed our supervisor's. This time it was a fellow caller, a Muslim medical student.

```
Re: URGENT: Calling Tonight
From: XXXXXXXXXXX
Sent: 07 July 2005 11:46:48
To: XXXXXXXXXXX
Cc: XXXXXXXXXX

Dear all,
hope your all safe and well.
I decided not to go to Russell square to my department
today this morning.Many of my friends in London
especially around the blast sites are missing still
- we know they left to get to work at that time, so
please keep them your thoughts.

regards,
XXX


Dear all,
A quick email to check that you are all OK. Due to the
current situation in London we have decided to cancel
the shift this evening. We will be telephoning those of
you who are down to attend tonight but PLEASE RESPOND
TO THIS EMAIL if you see this email before we reach
you by phone - we expect difficulty reaching you all by
telephone.>

Thanks,
XXX
```

In the weeks that followed the tragedy, the atmosphere in London was of fear and uncertainty, especially on the tube. There were many nights in which I'd lay awake, trying and failing to make sense of it all. No one could have fathomed this would happen in London, but we all felt vulnerable now. Still we were lucky; this was nothing compared to what citizens of war ravaged countries experienced, the unpredictability of whether they would survive to see another day and the constant reminder of their own mortality.

The first few days after the bombings, armed police stood guard at tube stations across the capital. When news broke that the explosions had been caused by Muslim suicide bombers from the UK, I could almost envisage a collective sigh from Muslims across the country. Great. Just what we needed, another group of nutters carrying out appalling acts in the name of our beloved faith. Their action was not the Islam I knew.

I was born and brought up in North Kensington, West London, to parents of mixed heritage who were raised in East Pakistan. I would describe my parents as practicing Muslims, I really dislike using terms such as 'moderate' or 'conservative' as they can be divisive and open to interpretation, after all, one man's moderate is another man's radical. It's ludicrous the way the government have used the term 'moderate' (now a widely used social term) as a euphemism for 'acceptable' Muslims. Categorising us will only further alienate individuals.

Islam definitely played a large part in my formative years, in that celebrating the Eids and Ramadans were very special times of the year, my older brother and I regularly attended Arabic class and we always ate halal food. Observing the peaceful prayers performed by my parents in the privacy of our home, the poetic beauty of the surahs recited from the Qur'an by my mother, and the excited hustle and bustle of Regent's Park Mosque on Eid morning are my earliest and fondest memories of the faith.

Then there's what my parents taught us; universal morals which form the basis of most religions, the emphasis on truth, honesty, being fair and respecting yourself and others. There was also a considerable emphasis placed on the importance of education, with my father helping to teach me how to read from an early age. These are the things my parents took from Islam and imparted to me and my two brothers. At primary school, I was soon dubbed the class bookworm. Back then as a child, never would it have occurred to me that people could one day associate my religion with bloodshed and murder.

Travelling into central London a few days after the bombings, on the Metropolitan line, I felt cautious. But looking around me, it was admirable to see the resilience of Londoners going about their daily lives, despite the nervous looks and tentative glances people gave each other. It made me sad to think that bearded and obviously Muslim-looking men were now regarded with fear and caution. I remember looking out of the tube window at Finchley Road and seeing two bearded Muslim men being stopped and searched by police offering up the contents of their plastic carrier bags and rucksacks. The men looked resigned to the fact that they had been targeted for obvious and understandable reasons.

9/11 had been disturbing and bewildering enough, and its impact on Muslim communities across the world was colossal. But it was only as I watched the men slowly being searched that I realised things had permanently changed for Muslims across the UK. Things would never be the same again. In recent times, never have one religion and its followers come under so much scrutiny and criticism, and it was down to the actions of an unrepresentative handful.

In the aftermath of the 7/7 bombings the social and political landscape of the country changed immeasurably. Five years on and Muslim communities are now fair game in the media, and targeted in various ways by the authorities. It appears our position is between a rock and a hard place.

The immediate impact of the attacks soon became apparent. Stories of women having their hijabs ripped off their heads and Muslims being spat on in the street were already making the news rounds. Mosques being vandalised and Muslim children being targeted in the playground followed. Islamophobia had been on the rise since 9/11 but now it was on our own doorstep, and going strong. But the real long term effects can only be viewed in retrospect. The disproportionate targeting of Muslim youths stopped and searched, the extraordinary rendition of suspected terrorists to the US, the government's introduction of its highly divisive anti-extremism programme 'Prevent', and a backlash against the hijab and niqab (face veil) are just a few examples of how things have developed and changed for the Muslim community.

And then there is the relentless debate on the 'position' of Muslim women in the UK. As if we were of another species. Oppressed, depressed and repressed is still the message projected by the media about us and our experiences — very few of our own voices are included in this public conversation, but speculation is widespread. Sons, fathers and brothers are talked about in terms of angry extremists, Muslim mothers, daughters and sisters are talked about in terms of needing to be 'saved' and 'liberated' from the 'shackles' of our headscarves and, more importantly, our religion. It is infuriating. Middle-class, middle-aged and predominantly white journalists and writers (many of them female) showed how very little they knew about Muslim women and the real issues they faced, beyond the sensationalisation of the hijab, demonstrated by their two dimensional portrayals of us in the media.

Then there was the question of how Muslim youths viewed themselves. The news that three of the four bombers were British Pakistanis was troubling to say the least. It appeared that the government did not know how to handle the idea that these men who were born and brought up here were willing to carry out such acts of terrorism on their homeland. And so ensued the wary debate about identity and how confused many Muslim youths had become. Was it their faith that came first, or their nationality, or perhaps it was their ethnic and cultural heritage?

For someone such as me, who was born in London, to Muslim parents of mixed South Asian, Afghan and African heritage, the answer was quite simple, really. I was a Londoner who was all those things, Muslim, British, Asian and more. I was one and all and I didn't like the idea of having to choose — but it felt like we had to prove we were not like the radicals who wanted to blow us all up.

Most recently the subject of the radicalisation of young people has turned to alleged extremism on university campuses when a Muslim student attempted to detonate a bomb in his underwear on a plane to Detroit, USA. Instead he ended up charring his own crown jewels and fortunately failed to hurt anyone else. It emerged he was an international student from Nigeria, who had studied at UCL and was president of the Islamic Society (ISoc) during my final year, 2006-2007. When this story broke, ISocs fast became implicated in radicalising students, and evoked a hysterical media furore. As a former member of UCL ISoc myself I found it extremely startling.

Following 7/7, despite the fact that I was the only Muslim girl in my department during my degree, and one of the three Asians in my year (the only of Pakistani ethnicity), the other two being boys, I felt no marked difference in peoples' behaviour towards me. There was certainly no open hostility from what I observed around campus, and I continued attending ISoc events organised by the society. Thinking back now to my experience, I saw no 'indoctrination' of attendees or guest speakers inciting extremism. From what I remember, there were many talks organised around international issues such as Palestine and the war in Iraq, but these talks had an open door policy so everyone was invited to attend. They were widely publicised and there was nothing insidious about them. But most people who attended these talks were Muslims, with the odd philosophy student who had an interest 'in all religions'.

Admittedly, I only came into contact with male students from the ISoc at these events and I don't recall ever meeting Abdulmutallab, but I do not believe that UCL was where the seeds of his extremist views and actions were sown. It was a perversion of Islam to think killing innocent people was a justified means of attacking the West and I had never heard any student Muslim or otherwise say anything of the like, either in close circles, or when addressing an audience.

It's clear that a minority of Muslims have interpreted Islam in a very twisted way. What I do accept is that such views exist and it is a real problem among a small minority of young Muslims, particularly men, who for a number of complex and misguided reasons feel moved to kill innocent civilians to make their point. I have quite honestly never directly witnessed radicalisation; my experience of this is only through what has been reported in the media. I've only heard the hate preached by tin pot clerics and imams on the news, and read their quotes in the papers, but in my everyday life as a Muslim I have not come across any individual or group like this.

Could this be because London is so different from other cities across the UK? I wasn't so sure. Maybe it was more because the young people most affected by radical Muslim rhetoric were disenfranchised youths from closed communities who felt there was no other way to express their outrage at the injustices against Muslim communities across the world but to blow themselves up among innocents.

A lot of it is down to mistaken notions of justice for the 'Ummah', the Muslim community. For the general non-Muslim public, it can be hard to distinguish the views and actions of an individual from the faith community he or she belongs to, and is acting in the name of. I just pray one day, someday soon we are no longer treated as the 'other', because we are not so different; our struggles, hopes and fears are the same as everyone else's and as universal as love.

THE RAGE
& THE FEAR

YASER IQBAL

Yaser Iqbal is a barrister living and practicing law in Birmingham. He came to the UK in 1986 as young boy. He was a British national since birth but had never set foot on UK soil till then. He lived in Azad Kashmir in Pakistan where he spent his early childhood.

"... if anyone slays a human being unless it be [in punishment] for murder or for spreading corruption on earth – it shall be as though he had slain all mankind; ..."

Quran 5:32

I CAN still vividly recall the menace and hatred in the eyes of almost every white face that stared at me on that day – and they all stared. I was in Gravesend, in Kent. The Muslims are a small minority there. A man drove past with his family in the car and was looking at me with a look of disgust, as if to say: "How could you?" I offered a smile but it made no difference. Usually, the folk of this small English town were quite friendly. A white van drove past, it slowed, and two sets of furious eyes glared at me – good job I'm in a car, I thought.

I completely understand why I had received the sentiments I did that day from those people. Further, I also appreciate what the non-Muslim population of this nation must have felt as a whole; the rage, the contempt, the mistrust and maybe even fear. I say this because initially, when it started early that morning, I felt the same way. The hair on the back of my neck was standing as news reeled in about the explosions in the capital. We were being attacked!

The wound inflicted on the character of Islam by the happenings of 11 th September 2001 had barely closed when all of a sudden this happened. The damage caused by 9/11 was bad enough without the events of 7 th July 2005 inflicting further damage to Muslims' relations with the rest of the world. This was not good. I recall the sheer helplessness with a hint of panic that I felt in the days after the fateful events; I had heard reports of Muslims being sidelined and facing hatred in the United States and was dreading the same happening in the United Kingdom – my own country, my home.

As the days unfolded, I listened to assault after assault from the various sources of the media. The news channels, the newspapers, the radio and the internet – the message being sent out was clear, it was not expressly stated but was very strongly implied; Muslims were public enemy number one, we were terrorists, suicide bombers. Hating us was the flavour of the month, so as to speak. The fact that several innocent lives were lost on that day and the fact that what happened was an assault on Adam-kind as a whole was bad enough. However, what followed was not very noble either. The media acted ruthlessly and irresponsibly in severing Muslims' relations with the world. They portrayed us as being evil. How dare they! I was enraged.

My contribution to this book commences with an extract of a verse from the Qur'an which we Muslims believe is the last testament from God. The Almighty's words are irrefutable; to kill an innocent human being is equated to the killing of the whole of mankind. It does not only say to not kill an innocent Muslim, but to not kill a human being – be he a Muslim, Christian, Jew, Hindu, Sikh, Buddhist or anything else. Our Lord teaches us the value of one human life. It is as precious as the whole of mankind. This verse in the Qur'an finishes by saying that the opposite is also true. To save one life is to save the lives of the whole of mankind. So not only did the God that we Muslims kneel down to five times a day clearly tell us that it is forbidden to take an innocent life but he taught us how precious a life is. I have not come across any other philosophy or doctrine that places such an immeasurable value on just one life, as does God in that one verse of the Qur'an.

My knowledge is rather limited in that I am unable at this time to cite other authorities from the Qur'an or from the sayings of our beloved prophet, the messenger of God, Muhammad, that specifically condemn the murder of innocent people. However, I do know the basics as I have stated in the preceding paragraph and I know that such acts are forbidden in Islam. The people who lost their lives on that day were all innocent men, women and children. This is true of the casualties of all terrorist attacks.

It is clear in my mind, as it was at that time, that there is no scope for the murder of an innocent person in Islam. What I found to be infuriating was the fact that the media peddled the opposite message. The media portrayed Islam and the Muslims in an extremely negative light fuelling the anti-Islamic sentiments. I found this to be very unfair in the least and considered it to be outright irresponsible and wrong. The people who in effect are the media are all educated, at least graduate-calibre, eloquent, talented and knowledgeable people who are seasoned at seeking out the truth from a given situation and presenting all sides of an argument. I am not just referring to the truth behind the perpetrators' true motives and real affiliations but rather more specifically to the truth of the creed I was speaking of earlier: that there is no scope for killing innocent people in Islam. Our journalists probably know this. Then why did they not spread this message out to the masses? Why did every report and every bulletin carry the same disinformation message?

These people knew that Muslims form a substantial part of many communities in the UK. People from our faith are spread out in almost all spheres of life in the UK. Was it never thought that liberally using the terms 'Islamic militants' or 'Muslims terrorists' would incite community disharmony? No-doubt, I was disgusted at the people who were behind the events of 7/7, but I do not hold in great esteem the journalists of the day either. Of course, their crime is not as heinous as that of the terrorists but it is nevertheless a crime in my view. These people did a responsibility to ensure that the actions of a select demented few do not spill-over to create disharmony between the Muslims and the rest of society.

Yes, there were intermittent comments to the effect that these acts do not represent the view of Muslims as a whole etc. However, these were over-shadowed by the general message against Muslims. It was the media that piped endless propaganda to assassinate the character of the message of Islam and of those who follow it. I knew at that time that 7/7 would be very damaging to Muslims in this regard. However, I was not to know the true extent of it till a few years on. I came across many non-Muslim people after this time who actually hold Muslims responsible for 7/7. I have said before that the perpetrators of 7/7 did not portray any Muslim sentiment and they were certainly not following the message of Islam when they murdered innocent people on that day.

I can give some examples of people whom I have encountered who have brought some dismaying truths home. I recall helping out at a friend's shop wherein a slightly tipsy, middle-aged white man started to talk about things he probably normally would not talk about but alcohol perhaps had the better of him. Subsequent to some banter between some Muslims in the shop and him, he said "Yeah, you lot are alright though you know. I can understand why you lot did it..." he then proceeded to justify (perhaps to himself) why we, the Muslims, blow people up and he blamed the government for having waged a war in Iraq. Initially I did take a tongue-in-cheek attitude to this scenario and found it rather amusing. This poor chap was actually starting to get emotional about what he perceived to be the fact that here we were, Muslims, who can be such a jovial bunch who love a bit of banter and a laugh and yet here we also were having to blow people and things up because our government was at war with a Muslim nation. It was all the government's fault and he understood where we were coming from! My amusement was short-lived because I came to realise that many people in this country believe that ordinary Muslims such as me were behind 7/7.

This was truly shocking. I then encountered Muslims who believed this also. Young, educated and every-day Muslims, who felt that it was Muslims like us who must have murdered innocent people on 7/7. This was around the time when the anti-terrorist legislation was passed in the UK. Whilst I was putting my hippy hat on and getting all annoyed at the potential for breach of civil liberties implicit in the new legislation, someone I knew was of the view that good Muslims had nothing to worry about because they were not terrorists and that it was only those who were terrorists who should be worried. He then went about his business, apologetic about something which Muslims did not do. I wanted to bang my head against the wall.

What I am trying to say here is that as the years rolled by I came to realise that a huge majority of people in this country and indeed all over the world believe that ordinary every-day Muslims were behind 9/11 and 7/7. The media has done a great job of convincing people that Abdul next-door could easily wake up tomorrow morning, strap on a bomb that he made in the garage from ingredients he purchased from B&Q, and blow himself up on the bus to work. It is outrageous and sad that intelligent people all over the country could be so easily led to hold such naïve views. Terrorists have existed for most part of the latter half of the last century but never before have the people lived in such doubt and fear of them and never before has the word terrorism been associated to one creed and doctrine like it is being done today. The extent of the general ignorance of people when it comes to having an informed understanding of the world around them beggars belief. It is books such as this one that will, hopefully, play a vital role in curbing this prevailing ignorance.

What is needed here is a deeper understanding of the modern world and its key players at a global level. I am not pointing towards some conspiracy theory but what I am presenting is my view that the explanation as to the real perpetrators of 7/7 is not as simple as most people are led to believe.

Take a moment to consider the following. Some things just do not add up when it comes to 7/7. The same was true of 9/11. Use your own intellect and reasoning and think about how it takes months of strategic planning by experts meticulously studying the blue prints of any building in order to effect a demolition of it whereby upon detonation of the carefully placed explosives the building will collapse onto itself such that it will not damage anything else in the vicinity. Then consider how it, apparently, only took the flying of two planes into the World Trade Centre towers to get the same result. Why is so much time taken by demolition experts who have undergone so much training to do the job at hand when they can just fly a remotely controlled airplane into a building requiring demolition? The simple answer is because that is not what happened on 9/11. I must emphasize that I am not some conspiracy buff but what I am propagating is pure logic and simple facts. One can study matters into even more depth but even when applying the simplest of logic one can understand that something is definitely very off-key here.

Now consider this also. I was watching ITV news on the day of the 7/7 attacks at around 8pm. It was a live interview with Peter Power who I later came to know to be the Managing Director for a private firm called Visor Consultants (a company that provides training exercises for organisations to teach them to deal with real emergencies). He was saying that on that day his company was providing a training exercise to a client company using exactly the same scenario that had actually taken place and that it was all an amazing coincidence. The actual news report is available on the internet to view and below is a small excerpt of the interview:

> POWER: Today we were running an exercise for a company – bearing in mind I'm now in the private sector – and we sat everybody down, in the city – 1,000 people involved in the whole organisation – but the crisis team. And the most peculiar thing was we based our scenario on the simultaneous attacks on an Underground and mainline station. So we had to suddenly switch an exercise from 'fictional' to 'real'. And one of the first things is, get that bureau number, when you have a list of people missing, tell them. And it took a long time –
>
> INTERVIEWER: Just to get this right, you were actually working today on an exercise that envisioned virtually this scenario?
>
> POWER: Er, almost precisely. I was up to 2 o'clock this morning, because it's our job, my own company, Visor Consultants, we specialise in helping people to get their crisis management response. How do you jump from 'slow time' thinking to 'quick time' doing? And we chose a scenario – with their assistance – which is based on a terrorist attack because they're very close to, er, a property occupied by Jewish businessmen, they're in the city, and there are more American banks in the city than there are in the whole of New York – a logical thing to do. And it, I've still got the hair on the back of my neck standing up...

> (http://www.julyseventh.co.uk/july-7-terror-rehearsal.html)

This was aired on live TV throughout the nation. Readers may watch the clip on the internet and see for themselves. After this time, it was never shown on TV again and this issue with Peter Power and the company who gave him this "exact scenario" was never heard of again or discussed or investigated. It is not just me but countless others who watched this piece of the news. The question we must ask is that why was this issue never investigated by the police? In a situation such as the one on 7/7 would it not have made perfect sense to investigate any leads that may explain who was behind the murder of several British citizens? The link, I feel, is too incriminating to be ignored as being a mere coincidence. Why were Peter Power and the company which devised this 'fictional scenario', which suddenly became real on that same day and at that same time, never questioned by the police? Could it be that the real perpetrators planned this such that if they were caught or arrested in the commission of their role in the terrorist attack they could just say that they were part of a training exercise? Why did the media not mention this information? Any person with an iota of common sense can see that something is very wrong here.

What is very interesting is that subsequent to 7/7, the Prevention of Terrorism Act 2005 and the Terrorism Act 2006 were passed through parliament and became law in the UK. These Acts serve to almost eliminate the rights of any individuals.

There are about 1.5 billion Muslims in the world. That is about 2 out of every 6 people in the world. If Islam really was a religion of terror do you not think there would be much more of it? The fact is that Muslims are just like every other person – we are peaceful and peace loving. Practicing Muslims adhere to a high code of moral and social conduct. The myth created in the modern world against Muslims needs to be dispelled and I feel that it needs to be done so by educating people about Islam and by Muslims themselves acting as ambassadors of their faith.

Like other Muslims in this country, I see the UK as my home. I support England in the World Cup; I like Jaguars because they represent some of the best in British motoring – well, they used to! I am proud of the fact that we have the best national health service in the world (incidentally, a national health service is an idea which Islam introduced over 1400 years ago) and I love the fact that we have the freedom to practice our religion as we wish. We Muslims are people like everyone else here with similar routines and similar problems in our lives. The people who perpetrated 9/11 and 7/7, whether they used patsies or however they did it, are enemies of us all and we need to stand united against them and ensure that we promote increased harmony in our communities for a peaceful future. We must educate our children to love and respect our fellow human beings for therein lies the greatest good.

IN SEARCH OF
HORIZON

SHAHIDA AHMED

Shahida Ahmed is a teacher, artist and a presenter on Ummah TV, an Islamic television station based in Blackburn. As a local Councillor, she is involved in various community initiatives. She is also the CEO of the Qur'an Project, a UK based initiative that aims to complete a hand written Qur'an in the United Kingdom. She is a single mother, bringing up three teenage children.

AS a young person born in Nelson, home meant my surroundings, my family, school and college. My friends at school were all from white British backgrounds and at the time 'white British' was something I was unaware of because my friends were just friends, not a colour or a faith. Sadly, in 1989 I lost a beautiful friend Lisa, who died of cancer and my uncle suffered a brain haemorrhage, which affected our family business Shahzad Textiles. Having been exposed to tragedy at such a young age provoked many questions in my head. My friend was cremated and I wondered what would happen if my uncle never pulled through his ill health; how would he be buried? I was unaware of my belief as a Muslim, and the practicalities and the meaning of Islam other than Salah or recitation of the Qur'an in Arabic. My parents were wonderful people. My father always left home in his western clothes; I remember my mother asking him "Are you ashamed to wear your shalwar kameez when you go out?" His standard reply was something like, "I live in England and when I go out it's respectful to wear what everyone else is wearing and when I am home I can wear whatever I wish."

Home was a place where I cooked daily, learned to sew and make things. The community was very close knit, it had Aunty Valerie, Aunty Suriyah and many other 'aunties'. My beloved mother was a dynamic, hard working lady who supported my father with the family business and also managed nine children. Today the thought of nine children is a mere fear of financial burden or impracticality. I smile thinking of times when my mum said "When you get married and have a family you will learn that a woman has to have all skills, and if she has a lot of skills she will be a better mother, daughter, sister and wife." At that time I thought "Yes, whatever!"

Most of our family friends were from Pakistan. Lancashire had a huge pool of ethnic minorities who had come for the labour market and the many cotton factories in Pendle and Burnley.

UNIVERSITY

In 1989 I left home for a journey where I was exposed to the 'real world', not the protected shelter of the life in our home that I led in a small town in Lancashire called Nelson. It is an amazing town, full of green hills and a varied landscape; every time I travelled away from home I missed the sheep, the cows, the smell of manure and the beautiful daffodils. It wasn't until I was away from it all that I could see home as a place of natural beauty. In Punjabi maybe we could call Nelson a 'pind' (village).

I went to Leeds University (Bretton Hall) based in Yorkshire Sculpture Park. It was the first time in my life I was alone without the shelter of my parents. This was also an experience that taught me how to get on a bus. One day sitting under a beautiful oak tree, I was writing one of my many poems on belonging and placement. I was away from my home and my mind started to think and ask questions, albeit without many answers. The students on the campus were mainly non Muslims and my questions were on my faith and my culture which I could not expose openly. My clothes, traditional shalwar kameez, stood out as being very different. I realized that my upbringing and identity were different from that of all my peers. Home, the place I remembered, was my place of belonging and now I was not belonging. South Asian dress was, for me a norm because my mother made a good effort to ensure that we had our cultural identity. Although my dad hesitated to wear traditional clothes I think for the females it was more the fact that they never really wore western clothes in those days. I was very comfortable with my hybrid identity and never conscious of what I wore at all. In fact I loved wearing my Liberty designer clothes from Lahore. Lahore was the centre of fashion in Pakistan and it made you feel, well, 'in'.

Being 'Muslim'

The first big 'Muslim' event that I recall was the first Gulf War. In all the hostels the students were glued to what was happening. Words like bombing, war, Iraq, oil, Saddam, invasion, Kuwait and Baghdad were perpetually echoing in the corridors of university hostels. Amid these unfamiliar words, my peers started to say "You're Muslim." I was already asking myself question about my belonging and now I was wondering what 'Muslim' meant? All of a sudden I was 'Muslim' more than before, but I wasn't about war, greed for oil and blood. So where in Islam was all this and why were Muslims fighting? My friends started asking me many questions about my faith and how it was brutal and how we Muslims fought with each other. I regularly heard "Well with no offence Shahida, we don't mean you, you're one of us." What was "One of us?" It was also during this time I went to Pakistan and got engaged. This was my first visit to the country, and my mum must have gone after a gap of a good 20 years.

Married Life

Nearly a decade later, I was a mother, wife and teacher; teaching Year 6 at St John's, a small Church of England school in Stacksteads, Bacup, Lancashire. Stacksteads was a very traditional area of white British people, many of whom had never left the valley. I was the only coloured face the children had been exposed to. Come to think about it, I was often the only brown face in many situations. One thing I vividly remember about this school was a little Year 2 girl starring at me non-stop. That day was the only day I had decided not to wear western clothes but instead traditional ones just to show the kids how beautiful they can look in the summer. My mother didn't mind western clothes; she used to always say "Wear what you want when you get married." So while teaching for practical reasons I wore western clothes. The Year 2 girl was still looking. As I walked past her I remember her saying "Miss, what planet do you come from?" That was a very profound moment for me as I realised that she had never seen anyone coloured or anyone dressed differently, so for her I was an alien. I giggled and said to her "The same one as you my dear." So, imagine being in Stacksteads at the time of 9/11, where people have only ever been exposed to one Muslim, a 'Muslim teacher'. As the news flashes constantly referred to 'the Muslims' and 'Muslim terrorists', I contemplated whether this term 'Muslim' referred to me or to someone else. I also realised that the people of Stacksteads only had me as a reference point to the term 'Muslim'.

Often, when they used the term during their discourse of the 9/11 events with me, they would add something like "Shahida with no offence to you but you know what we mean." In other words, they expressed a very negative stereotype of all Muslims, that is apart from myself. After such a long time I felt that once again I would be questioned about who I am and what my faith was. This time the difference was that, as a mother, I realized my children were exposed to something far earlier than I had been. Their friends were all white British; how would they be looking at them or wanting to know things. Would I have to start explaining to them who they were? Actually who were they; British, Muslim, Pakistani? They had three different identifications from birth.

Following 7/7, my daughter came home with a rather bizarre statement by her Religious Education (RE) teacher about jihad and how Muslims killed for faith. My daughter was one of two Muslim girls in her year group at a high school which was situated in a very conservative Yorkshire castle town. This made me aware of the difficulty my child might have in responding to her peer group. Her anger was evident in her question "Mum, why are Muslims killing?" The word jihad was exploited; something I had never heard of or been taught in my RE lessons. The climate of religion that children were now being exposed to in schools had started to change.

CREATIVE JOURNEY

In 2005 four Muslim men, three from Yorkshire, near a location where my children were studying, carried out terrorist attacks, and this time the target was nearer, not the Gulf, not America, but London! The rhetoric on TV with phrases such as 'Muslim Terrorists' was all too familiar. However, this time I trembled as these attacks were close to home. I again became conscious about my faith, my belonging, and how people saw me this time.

In addition, 7/7 also emphasized new terminology such as 'Islamophobia, 'extremism' and 'Prevent'. These words penetrated from the top into the grassroots communities. Words which, through work, I came across and got angry with as they were exploited to provide streams of funding to deal with 'terrorism' and involved ticking streams of boxes to say we had dealt with it. I worked unpaid with the voluntary sector and had learned since 2005 how systems worked with government initiatives, community groups and political agendas. The people that really mattered were those who faced daily issues like poor housing, health and work problems.

When I left teaching after my father's death and worked at grassroots level, I discovered the real problems and issues faced by people. They were not about war and terrorism. For them it was lack of inspiration, deprivation and education. I saw many women in a hijab and abaya from Muslim communities, Muslim men with beards. Was it because of the events that took place or because they feared an identity crisis? Whilst working on a project on Minaj-ul-Quran Radio (a station run by an international Muslim organisation), I was approached to do a show for women. At the time I thought "No way – me radio? No!" When I was asked again, I thought I should not be negative and maybe should do something positive for my community. I started a series of programmes on Muslim leadership in the world and role models. People started listening and responding, a dialogue started shaping up as issues were being raised about the community. Women were raising many questions about Islam and culture. Islamophobia did not matter to them, as much as unemployment and domestic violence.

Working with children, women and the community made me realise that many internal issues needed attention and that many Muslim women were still not accepted in their own communities. What became important to me was my role in the community I lived in. In 2008, I became Nelson's first Muslim female independent town councillor. For me what now mattered was not national agendas but local grassroots issues and how we needed to educate children and women and create opportunities for them to engage and be heard. I discovered that I could do this through art. My art work was traditional Islamic art which represented the history of Muslims around the world and their achievements. Through it, I gained inspiration and shared a positive message of how people from different faiths lived together. However, I realised that I was just a minute grain of sand in a huge world and what I did alone would only make a minimal change. I also knew that my faith taught me not to criticise but to move forward with progression.

ACTIONS, REACTIONS & NEW DIRECTIONS

AHMED BASHIR

Ahmed Bashir is a Policy Adviser at Her Majesty's Treasury, where he has worked for a number of years. He is a Chartered Management Accountant and sits on the Chartered Institute of Management Accountants Central Government Committee. Ahmed has previously worked at the Ministry of Justice and the Department for Work and Pensions and is currently Chair of the Civil Service Islamic Society a non-political, voluntary society, representative of mainstream Islamic opinion in Central Government.

IT was a beautiful day in Brighton. I remember sitting in a conference room contemplating the warmth of the outdoors. I was totally oblivious to the catastrophe unfolding in rush hour London that day.

I was listening to the course tutor discussing changes to the tax system, when my phone began to vibrate, and it was phone call after phone call and a deluge of text messages coming through. I had forgotten to charge my phone the night before, but just before the battery died I read a text from my brother, asking "Are you OK?" It was unusual for my brother to text me randomly and ask how I was. I noticed that a few of my colleagues were also checking their phones; then one of them nudged me and whispered that there had been an explosion in London.

Of course the thought that a terrorist attack had happened and that, too, in the heart of London, of all places, was inconceivable. Therefore, I was unable to grasp the true extent of the news. After the conference, I went back to the hotel room and charged my phone to ring home. My family was ecstatic to hear from me; they had all gathered at my parent's house waiting for my call. My mum explained how worried they had all been and how she had felt sick with the worry of not knowing whether I was dead or alive. I was relieved to bring them comfort, confirming I was safe and sound.

I switched on the television and was taken aback by what I saw. The tube stations I travel in and the buses I rely on had been attacked. I was deeply saddened for those that had been injured and my heart went out to those that had lost loved ones. I thought about what the crying mothers, searching brothers and the waiting sisters would be feeling. I remember picturing myself as the one dying in the deep tunnels and what I would be feeling and what I would want to say to my loved ones. Years later I pictured myself in this situation again whilst writing some of my poetry, in particular a poem titled "Awaiting thee".

I felt lucky in that I had not travelled that morning and had decided to leave the day before, but I regretted not being there to help neighbours and colleagues. This feeling, together with the desire to help, was to result in my later training as a St John's Ambulance First Aider.

Faced with the reality of such atrocity I considered "What if? What if I was on the train and my life had ended?" Such thoughts pushed me to think about life from a different angle, how I would want to be remembered, to live life to the full and not postpone what I keep meaning to do.

When I finally got back to work, things were different; people were talking about what had gone on. There was a lot of discussion amongst people about Islam and how these attacks were perpetrated in the name of Islam. Many non-Muslim friends and colleagues asked me about how Islam promoted such behaviour. The interest shown was very much in my view, a genuine desire to learn more about Islam, and to try and see how terrorism could be in any way associated to the religion of Islam.

I was keen to explain the peacefulness of Islam; I drew on my own experience of Muslims around me, mainly family and friends. A lot of the questions I received focused on why, in a peaceful religion, people with such thinking can justify their acts as being within the confines of Islam. I found it difficult to answer the questions as fully as I would have wanted to, I focused on the argument that there are bad eggs in every community and these people will look for anything to legitimise their actions.

I found that there were gaps in my knowledge and I needed to learn more about Islam. This realisation made me understand to some extent how others in my situation who have a weak understanding of the inner details of Islam, can be led down a variety of different paths if they rely on a single teacher. I found from my own study and evaluation of the views amongst the different strands of Muslims that one needs to keep an open mind, question and challenge any information with basic principles of fairness, piety, etc. on which Islam is built and how these principles match with what one may be told.

I remembered the time I was at university and how I had then encountered fellow Muslims who had very different Islamic views from my own and those around me. There was no engagement or discussion with these individuals as they were very argumentative and confrontational which led people to avoid them, rather than to engage and challenge them. These individuals also came across as very educated in Islam, whereas I and the majority of others lacked Islamic knowledge and understanding. However when I look back, engagement and challenge was necessary not only to open the minds of others to different perspectives but to open my own mind and to enhance my own knowledge. I think Muslims at university today need to be brave in engaging and challenging the different Islamic views they encounter during their university years. This can be done through the formation of debating societies made up of Muslims from all walks of life, the wider the diversity of participants, the better the debates and better learning and opening of the minds to different perspectives of thinking.

That year, July 7th changed things for everyone in the UK, but in particular for Muslims. My friend was attacked in the street whilst pushing her baby in a pram, racist language was used and the innocent baby was punched, all because my friend wore a head scarf. I had flashbacks of when I was younger, of times long gone, when petrol was poured through letterboxes because we were different. There was now a great sense that people did not understand that Islam was a peaceful religion and the media portrayed the ideology of a few as if it was that of the majority.

My dad would shout at the television in frustration due to the way Islam was portrayed, and at some of the messages put out by Muslims in the media. My mum would plan ahead of such frustration and change the television channel or focus attention elsewhere. I understood my father's frustration and was concerned that some of the people put forward to represent Muslims in the media were actually not representative of the Muslim diversity in our communities. The concerns were shared by many of my friends and the consensus was that there was a need for a body representative of the diverse Muslims in the UK, which would unite in a single consensus voice and a single message. We also understood the reality of this in that agreement between the various Muslim strands was a difficult prize to win. To this day, Muslim communities in Britain have difficulty in agreeing to celebrate Eid on the same day.

I remember feeling that I must do something to change things, to make things better. I felt it was important for me to try and raise awareness of Islam. To show that Islam is not what some media portrayed it to be. I spoke with fellow Muslims at work about how they were feeling and what they too were experiencing. We became a support group for each other; the collective which wanted to do something in order to make a difference resulted in the birth of the Civil Service Islamic Society.

The Civil Service Islamic Society aimed to represent mainstream Muslim opinion in Central Government, drawing on the diversity of Muslims within Government. The mission was to raise awareness of Islam, influence areas of Muslim interest and empower Muslim staff. The society was endorsed by the Cabinet Secretary, the Head of the Home Civil Service, Sir Gus O'Donnell and the Society was proud to have him as its patron.

The society began with awareness events and I remember my surprise at the attendance at the first event. The turnout was very high. There was a genuine want by people to learn about Islam and what it was really about; a lot of people used the opportunity to ask questions and learn as much as they could.

As the years have passed, the Society has held talks and Q&As with leading scholars allowing policy leads to question them, held networking events and has to some degree contributed to the formulation of Government policy that impacts Muslims. Some of the successes to date have been the establishment of a number of prayer rooms and 'wudu' facilities in Government department buildings and the provision of management guidance on religious leave, Ramadan, and prayer times. In addition, the society has also provided guidance and advice to help understand faith issues, such as dress codes, and has also developed a mentoring programme to help Muslims with career progression.

The events of 2005 have also resulted in other changes in me, in that I think more about what I do with my life and am thankful for what I have. Since 2005, I feel that people around me have a lot more understanding of Islam than in 2005, but there are still some misconceptions.

Going forward as a whole I think our Muslim communities need to open their eyes and challenge some of the messages some imams put out. There is a need for Muslims to unite and work together. I appreciate that everyone will have their own ideas as to how best the Muslim community should move forward and be improved. I know there is work being carried out successfully in some areas, but my suggestion, briefly put, is that firstly there needs to be a coming together of a broad set of Muslim leaders representative of the diverse Muslim communities in Britain which can speak with one voice. I think the success of this requires the diplomacy of a very good impartial chair.

Secondly, this body needs to engage with all mosques and enforce some form of self-regulation that is to set out a code of practice for mosques which promotes fair and transparent, democratically elected mosque leadership and clear criteria to the appointment of imams. There needs to be a lot more accountability and rights of the Muslim community to challenge. Mosques are not just places of worship but also community hubs, places of help, support and education and hence need to function this way. Mosques are also the apparatus of wider community engagement and building relationships, for example each mosque has a kitchen; why not use the kitchen to help all those in need in the wider community via soup kitchens?

Lastly, the Muslim communities need to be a component in decision-making, they need to elect their mosque leaders, have a say in the choice of imams and the running of mosques. The election of the body that regulates the mosque needs to be fair and transparent; the work they do needs to be communicated to communities and be consulted upon.

کی لند ن   A LAST POEM
نظم آخری   FOR LONDON

MURTAZA SHIBLI

۲۰۰۵ اگست ۲۵   25 AUGUST 2005

میری جان وفا افسوس اب میں لکھ نہیں سکتا
تراشے تیری باتوں کرے ، کوئی نغمے محبت کے
نہ کوئی بات گل کی، گلستاں کی، گل بداماں کی
نہ ہی باد صبا کی، رنگ و بو کی ، رنگ رلیوں کی
مجھے افسوس ہے جانم!
ہمارے شہر کے حاکم نے یہ فرمان بھیجا ہے
نہ کوئی سوچ سکتا ہے، نہ کوئی بول سکتا ہے
گوارا ہی نہیں اسکو کہ کوئی اسکی رعیت سے
کہے کچھ بات جو اسکی طبیعت پر گراں گزرے
سنا ہے اب تو ہر منزل
ہر اک راہ گزر، راہ وفا ، راہ تمنا پر
مرے جمہور کے غازی سپاہی سینہ تانے ہیں
وہ رکھیں گے نظر ہم پر، خبر رکھیں گے سوچوں کی
ہماری زندگی کے ہر کسی پہلو کو تا کیں گے
درازیں دل کی گہری ہیں مگر پھر بھی وہ جھانکیں گے

میری جان وفا افسوس صد افسوس ہے مجھ کو
ہمارے شہر کی رنگینیوں میں اب ملاوٹ ہے
دھندلکے شام کے بھاری، ہواؤں میں کراہت ہے
بہاریں خون کی پیاسی ہیں، جذبوں میں عداوت ہے
ہزاروں خوف انجانے فضاؤں میں لٹکتے ہیں
ہر اک جانب بھٹکتے ہیں، یہاں بدروح سائے ہیں
دلوں میں بال آیا ہے، مزاجوں میں بناوٹ ہے
اچانک ہر کوئی اپنا بھی اب انجان لگتا ہے
نہ جانے خیر کے سارے فرشتے کیوں مقیّد ہیں

Oh my faithful love, I can write no more

Fragments of our conversation, melodies of love

No more speak of flowers, rose gardens and flower bedecked dresses

No more morning breeze, scents, colours and dizzy dances

Alas! My love

The ruler of our destiny has decreed

That no one may utter words

Or even think forbidden thoughts

Not to his liking.

I hear that now every wayside place

Each lovelorn road, each highway of hope and alley of dalliance

Is patrolled by the warriors of prohibition,

Those appointed to keep us in their eye,

To follow our very thoughts

And spy into the deeps of our heart

Alas! My love, alas,

The elegant city has become desolate

Dusk lights heavy with fear, the air full of threats

A scent of blood on the wind, and hate in the dying sun.

Unspoken terrors beset us on every side

The shadows of dead souls pass through us

And our hearts are cracked, if not broken.

Suddenly all that is familiar is strange

And choirs that sang in harmony out of tune

ہر اک پھاٹک پہ داروغے، ہر اک آہٹ پہ پہرا ہے

ہر اک آواز میں جیسے عجب سی اک خموشی ہے

گھٹن سے منجمد ہے ہر کوئی منظر پریشاں ہے

ہر اک خنجر بکف ہے آستینوں میں تباہی ہے

ہر اک احساس کے اندر، ہر اک مسکان کے پیچھے

ہر اک چہرے سے جیسے بدگمانی سی جھلکتی ہے

مجھے لگتا ہے جیسے تاک میں آسیب بیٹھا ہے

تمّنا ؤں، خیالوں کے نہاں خانوں میں زنجیریں

ہلاکت خیز لمحے ہیں، زہر آلود تاثیریں

کوئی سوچے تو کیا سوچے ہوئی ہیں خاک تدبیریں

برے وقتوں میں رہتا ہوں نہ چھوڑیں ساتھ تدبیریں

کہیں اب میری نظموں کی بدل جا ئیں نہ تفسیریں

ہمارے شہر وحشت میں ہیں تعزیروں پہ تعزیریں

مجھے ڈر ہے بہت ڈر ہے کہیں اس شہر کا حاکم

جفاؤں کا یہ موسم ہے نہ ہو وہ بد گماں مجھ سے

میں بے اوقات کا شاعر خرابوں میں نہ گھر جاوں

مجھے اپنے خیالوں سے بہت ہی خوف آتا ہے

میری سوچوں کے تہ خانے، میرے خوابوں میں وحشت ہے

تمّنائیں ماوف ہیں ، مجھے اب بول آتا ہے

تخئیل میں اداسی ہے قلم اب کپکپاتا ہے

مجھے افسوس ہے جانم ، بہت افسوس ہے مجھ کو

The law stands guard at the entrance to our hearts

And every footfall is laden with a curious silence

We are suffocated by the dust of suspicion.

Every hand conceals a threat; the knife lies in every sleeve

Faces that smile seep suspicion

And the demon is awakened from his unquiet sleep.

The chambers of desire and longings are locked

Each moment is filled with apprehension

What can we make of plans that lie in ruins

Of these bad days that mark our fate

I fear for my poems, for if words change their meaning

Who knows what shapes our words will form

In this city stricken by terror.

I am afraid. For if the ruler of the city

In this season of oppression thinks my words are suspect,

I, the poet of low degree, may find myself punished

I am afraid of my own thoughts and feelings

The vaults of my thoughts and the dreams of my eyes are full of fear and dread

My desires are cancelled, terror has entered my heart

Fancy is dispirited and my pen is trembling

Alas my love...Alas!